101 CARD GAMES FOR ONE

101 Card Games For One

A COMPREHENSIVE GUIDE TO SOLITAIRE GAMES

BRENDA RALPH LEWIS

Random House
Puzzles & Games

NEW YORK   TORONTO   LONDON   SYDNEY   AUCKLAND

Published by Random House Puzzles & Games, an imprint of The Random House Information Group, a division of Random House, Inc., New York, and simultaneously in Canada by Random House of Canada Limited, Toronto.

RANDOM HOUSE is a registered trademark of Random House, Inc.

Please address inquiries about electronic licensing of any products for use on a network, in software or on CD-ROM to the Subsidiary Rights Department, Random House Information Group, fax 212-572-6003.

This book is available at special discounts for bulk purchases for sales promotions of premiums. Special editions, including personalized covers, excerpts of existing books, and corporate imprints, can be created in large quantities for special needs. For more information, write to Random House, Inc., Special Markets/Premium Sales, 1745 Broadway, MD 6-2, New York, NY 10019 or email specialmarkets@randomhouse.com

Visit the Random House Puzzles & Games Web site: www.puzzlesatrandom.com

First Edition

Printed and bound in Dubai

A catalog record for this title is available from the Library of Congress.

10 9 8 7 6 5 4 3 2 1

ISBN: 978-0-375-72234-9

Picture credits:
Mary Evans Picture Library: 6; Photos12.com: 7
All card diagrams © Amber Books Ltd

CONTENTS

INTRODUCTION

Solitaire, or Patience as it is known in some other parts of the world, is a family of card games. There are hundreds of different solitaire games, and each game may have many variations. The word *solitaire*, which is French for 'solitary', suggests that the lone card player has no opponents, but this isn't really true. In all the 101 games in this book, whether simple or complex, the opponent is the pack of cards itself, and the way chance operates to influence the outcome of the game.

L ike so many games, solitaire has its own jargon, though we've cut down on some of its more unusual words to ensure descriptions of how to play the game are as clear as possible. Some terms have been retained, however. For instance, the solitaire term 'tableau' – French for 'picture' – is used to describe the layout formed by dealing the cards at the start of a game. We've also kept the term 'foundation' for the cards that start the piles which should contain complete sequences at the end of the game. An 'exposed' card means one that is face up and not overlapped by another card. However, we have replaced the solitaire term 'packing' with 'placing' or 'building' to describe the way card sequences can be built up within the tableau before transfer to a 'foundation' pile. The solitaire term 'dealing to the center', which we have avoided in this book, doesn't literally mean what it says: in solitaire, the 'center' is the empty space above the tableau or layout.

The history of solitaire games

No one knows precisely when or where solitaire games were invented. Their introduction has often been ascribed to the French, because 17th century books on patience games mentioned references to solitaire in French literature. French origins are supported by a story that the former Emperor Napoleon Bonaparte played games of solitaire during his exile on the remote Atlantic island of St. Helena between 1815 and 1821, and by those games which have French titles, such as Le Cadran. The first modern collection of solitaire games appeared more recently, in around 1870, when Lady Adelaide Cadogan published her *Illustrated Games of Patience*.

Many of Lady Cadogan's solitaire games, and most of those devised since, have a common purpose. This is to re-order a pack of cards – or a double pack – into piles that follow the original sequence of a suit of cards. Most often, the piles run in ascending order from Ace to King, or in descending order from King down to Ace. But some, like Ninety-One, involve mental arithmetic. Others, like Hand, are simple games that rely on whichever cards you deal from a face down pack without knowing their suit, colour or rank (number).

Whatever their variations, all games of solitaire have their own particular virtue. Leslie Dodds, the British bridge champion and a member of the team that won the Bermuda Bowl at the Bridge World Championship in 1955, was a keen exponent of these intriguing games.

'Solitaire,' he once said. 'has all the restful beauty of solitude, combined with the stimulus of challenge.'

Above: The cover of a nineteenth-century book of patience games, translated from an original German edition by 'Professor Hoffman', a pseudonym of the magician Angelo John Lewis.
Right: Solo card games have been popular for several hundred years. This painting of a boy playing cards is by the French artist Jean-Baptiste-Siméon Chardin (1699–1779).

A BRIEF HISTORY OF CARDS AND CARD PLAYING

Cards and card playing have a long and tortuous history. Long, because many historians believe the earliest games go back more than one thousand years, to the ninth century. Tortuous, because no one really knows when playing cards were 'invented' or by whom.

The Chinese, who were using paper and, presumably, card from AD 100 are the most frequently cited candidates for the inventors of playing cards. But it is also probable that, like most aspects of social history, playing cards developed gradually in more than one society, in this case out of the great variety of games already devised in early cultures.

The first playing cards were hand-painted, and so expensive that only the wealthiest players could afford them. This monopoly was broken in Europe, where playing cards probably made their appearance in the 13th or 14th centuries, with the invention of woodcuts, which allowed cards to be mass-produced. As cards became cheaper to buy, sales rose and card playing became, as it remains, an integral feature of social life and leisure.

Cards were probably introduced into Europe from Egypt during the rule of the muslim Mamluks, who used the now-standard 52-card pack. This consisted of four suits comprising ten cards with 'pips' showing values one to ten and three court cards. Coming from such a source – Muslims and Christians were frequently at war throughout the Middle Ages – cards and card playing were soon condemned as dangerous and subversive.

Among their many critics were governments in cities like Regensburg in Germany and Florence in Italy, which attempted to ban cards or at least control their use. The chorus of disapproval was joined by individual churchmen with a puritan axe to grind. One was a Swiss monk, Johannes von Rheinfelden, who in 1377 described the suits used in card games recently arrived in Germany as as 'signifying evil'. Two centuries later, an English preacher called John Northbrooke was banging the same drum when he inveighed against the theatre and card playing as joint invitations to sin.

'The plaie at Cardes,' Northbrooke declared, 'is an invention of the devill, which he founde out, that he might the easier bring in idolatrie.'

Fashionable pastime

It was all a waste of time and breath. Cards and card playing had clearly come to stay, for as early as 1380, games were taking place in cities as disparate as Brabant, Paris, Barcelona and – despite official displeasure – Florence and Regensburg. More importantly, cards soon became a favourite sport for the leaders of fashion - the kings, queens, their officials and courts. With this endorsement, card playing became unstoppable as people of all classes followed the royal lead.

By 1590, designs for the 52-card pack were finalized in a form modern players could easily recognize. The major change from the early Mamluk pack involved the pictures used for the court cards. Islamic law forbade the making of images of living creatures – human or animal – so the Mameluke cards used abstract designs instead. In Christian Europe, where there was no such prohibition, the first court cards showed a King and two Marshals: the Marshals, who were high-ranking military officers, were later replaced by a Queen and a Knave (later Jack).

Rivalry arose over designs for the number cards. The Swiss favored flowers, bells, and acorns, the Germans preferred hearts, leaves, bells, and acorns. In Spain and Italy, card design featured swords, batons, cups, and coins. In addition, some unusual ideas were proposed, such as wine pots, drinking cups, books, and animals. All these designs had one great drawback: they came from drawings which had to be reproduced by expensive woodcuts. The so-called 'French suit' of hearts, diamonds, clubs, and spades, which won out over all the others, could be cheaply produced by stencils. These designs were also simpler and clearer when playing in dim light.

Artistic refinements

By this time, cards had become virtually an art form, and designers over the centuries continued to embellish them and also make them more convenient to use. Cards appeared in new shapes, including circular or oval variants. The more common rectangular cards acquired rounded corners. Early on, players had to use both hands to hold their cards in front of them with much of each card on display. After identifying marks were introduced at the corners and edges, one hand was sufficient. The first deck of this type was printed in about 1693.

A further innovation was the reversible or double-headed court card, in which the image was the same whichever way up the card was held. Previously, in earlier packs, the figures on court cards had been shown in full-length portraits. Card players were in the habit of reversing them, so giving

competitors notice of the cards they held. The new design, introduced in France in 1745, did away with this undue advantage but was immediately banned by the government. This may have been because it seemed insulting to the reigning monarch, Louis XV, to have card players holding their king upside down. However, the idea was taken up by card manufacturers in Italy and Spain, and, in 1799, in Britain. American card makers followed in 1802. The French, whose bloody revolution in 1789 had removed both their kings and their qualms about offensive royal images, finally adopted reversible court cards in 1827.

Decorative and practical

The backs of cards also received artistic attention. Initially plain and unvarnished, they acquired abstract designs, geometric patterns, portraits of famous people and even advertisements. In Britain, the ace of spades was put to similar use by governments. The ace, then simply the humble 'one', had first acquired special importance in the 15th century, when it was promoted from the lowest value card to a card that could rank highest in certain games. James I, who became King of England in 1603, devised his own use for it. The ace of spades was given an elaborate and fanciful design. The manufacturer's logo received the same treatment and the two together signified that tax had been paid on the cards. Imposing tax on British-made playing cards lasted for over 350 years, until 1960, but the fancy ace of spades is still a decorative feature for packs of cards today.

BLOCKADE

Like other solitaire games, such as Klondike (see page 77), the game of Blockade uses two packs of cards. And, just like Klondike, the aim of Blockade is to build card sequences on to eight foundations.

> **Equipment:** Two packs of playing cards
> **Rating:** Good chance to win
> **Level of Difficulty:** Easy

Setup

Deal 12 piles of one card each, face up. The other 92 cards form the stock. Put any dealt aces to the side, to create foundation cards, and replace them from the stock.

Playing the Game

Deal the cards one at a time, building on the foundations, by suit, in ascending order. Should aces become available, move them to the side to create foundation cards. You can also build on the tableau cards, by suit, in descending order. Individual cards or part-sequences can be moved from one tableau pile to another. When all the cards in a pile have been removed, leaving a space, fill it straight away with a card taken from your stock. Dealt cards that cannot be used should move to a waste pile, face up. The top card of the waste pile can be played at any time.

Finishing the Game

Continue dealing cards one at a time, placing cards on the piles or filling the spaces left by empty piles for as long as your stock of cards lasts. Once that happens, you can place any card or part-sequence of cards in any empty space that remains. There are no redeals in Blockade. If you have managed to move all 104 cards to the foundations, you have won.

Tableau for Blockade

BELEAGUERED CASTLE

Beleaguered Castle reflects medieval times when laying siege to castles was a regular feature of warfare. The purpose of Beleaguered Castle is to build up sequences of cards from aces to kings.

Equipment: A pack of playing cards
Rating: Easy to play, but hard to win
Level of Difficulty: Easy

Setup

Remove the four aces from the pack and arrange them in a central column. Shuffle the rest of the pack and deal further rows of six, with overlapping cards, to the left (the left wing) and to the right (the right wing) of the aces until the pack is used up.

Playing the Game

The aim is to build up the central foundations, from ace to king, ascending by suit. Only exposed cards, those on the far right and far left of the rows, are in play. You can move the exposed cards to form sequences on other exposed cards, descending, by suit. As you move a card away from the end of a row, a new card is exposed and comes into play. If you use up all the cards in one wing, you can put any card you want in the empty space.

Finishing the Game

The game is over when you can't move or if you've completed the foundation piles so that there's a king on the top of each and no walls left. There is a large element of chance to this game.

Tip

As you cannot put a king on top of any other wall cards, it is often useful to empty a wall of cards and put it there.

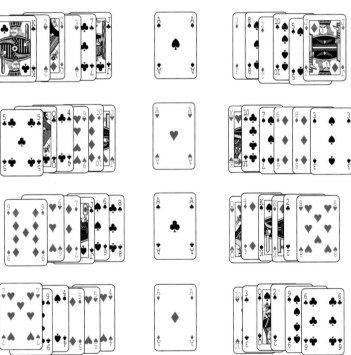

Tableau for Beleaguered Castle

CLOCK PATIENCE

The aim of Clock Patience is to arrange the cards into 13 piles, one for each hour of the clock. The thirteenth pile is called the 'king pile', because that is where all four of the king cards should be located at the end of the game.

Equipment: A pack of playing cards
Rating: Looks more complex than it is
Level of Difficulty: Easy

Setup

After shuffling the pack, deal the cards face down in a pattern like the hour hands of a clock, creating 12 piles of four cards each. The thirteenth pile of four (the 'king pile') should be placed in the middle of the 'clock', also face down.

Playing the Game

Pick the top card from the king pile and have a look at its rank. If it's a four, for example, place the card face up by the pile that occupies the four o'clock position on the clock face. Take the face-down card at the four o'clock position, look at

it, and place it by the position on the clock that it represents. Pick up the face-down card at that position and continue in this manner. If the card that you lift turns out to be a king, put it in the middle of the clock face, face up, and pick the next card in the king pile. Remember, the jack represents eleven o'clock and the queen, twelve o'clock.

Finishing the Game

A game of Clock Patience may end in one of two ways. In the first, you will finish with four cards of the same rank in each of the 13 piles of cards. That means you've won. Or if you have three kings in the central king pile and then turn up the fourth before you have completed the other piles, the game ends because no more moves are possible and, unfortunately, you've lost.

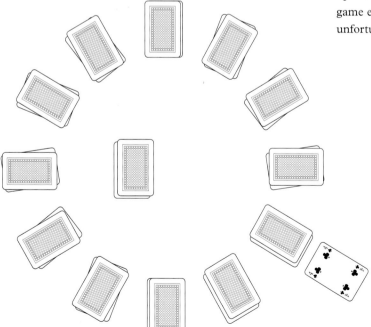

Playing Clock Patience

A completed game of Clock Patience

PRECEDENCE

Precedence, also known as Downing Street, has no tableau. The purpose is to end the game with all the cards built on their respective foundations in round-the-corner fashion, with a king placed over an ace, or an ace placed over a two and so on.

Equipment: Two packs of playing cards
Rating: Simple building game
Level of Difficulty: Easy

Setup

Take any one of the kings from the double pack and place it face up.

Playing the game

Deal the stock one at a time. As the cards appear, establish the other seven foundations in a left-to-right row in the following order: queen, jack, ten, nine, eight, seven and six. The cards can be of any suit. Start to build on the foundations in descending order, in any suit. If an ace is the top card on the foundations, then you round-the-corner to king, and so on until each foundation has 13 cards – i.e. the queen foundation ends with a king. However, you can't start building on a foundation until the foundation to the left has begun. If you can't use a dealt card, put it in a waste pile face up. You can use the top card of the waste pile for building purposes. When your stock of cards eventually comes to an end, turn the waste pile face down and start dealing again.

Finishing the Game

You can turn the waste pile over twice and redeal. When the stock runs out for the third time, the game is over. If you have eight sequences of 13 cards, you have won.

SIR TOMMY

There's a theory that Sir Tommy, also known as Try Again or Old Patience, is the original game of solitaire. In this game you construct ascending sequences from the ace to the king, not by suit or color, but by the numbers or value of the cards.

Equipment: A pack of playing cards
Rating: Piece of cake
Level of Difficulty: Easy

How to Play

Start by dealing the cards, one at a time. As an ace appears, place it, face up, as a foundation. You can now begin to build on this, in ascending order, using any suit. If you cannot use a card, place it into one of four waste piles, face up, beneath each of the four foundations. You can choose which card goes to which pile. If suitable, the top card of the waste pile can be used to build up the foundations. You cannot move cards between piles. Only one deal is allowed and the game is won when all cards have been used from the waste piles to build on the foundations. As you practice, you may find it helpful to reserve one waste pile for kings and high cards.

LABYRINTH

Many players believe the empty spaces give the tableau the look of a labyrinth, hence its name. The game can be protracted, because extra rows are continuously dealt to the tableau while you build ascending ace-to-king suit sequences.

> **Equipment:** A pack of playing cards
> **Rating:** Don't be fooled by the tortuous name of this game
> **Level of Difficulty:** Easy

Setup

Take the four aces from the pack and set them out in a row of foundation cards. Beneath them, deal eight cards, face up, in a row and place any cards that can help make an ascending suit sequence on the foundations. Fill the gaps in the eight-card row from the stock immediately.

Playing the Game

When you can no longer use this row, deal another row of eight cards below the first. As before, cards from this new row that contribute to sequences are placed on the foundations, but this time, don't fill the spaces that are left in the new row. When you can continue no longer, build another row. You can build a maximum of six rows. You can only place cards on the foundations if they are in the top or bottom rows. When a card has been played from the top row, the card immediately below it is available for play. When a card from the bottom row is played, the card above it is now available. Don't fill gaps in the top row after the first deal.

Finishing the Game

Continue until your stock of cards has run out. You have won the game if you have built all four foundations from aces to kings. If the game comes to a halt before this time, you can restart it by taking a card from anywhere on the tableau and placing it on a foundation.

A game of Labyrinth in progress

SIX BY SIX

Six by Six, which takes its name from the rows and columns in its tableau, is a straightforward single-pack game in which you have to build ascending ace-to-king sequences by suit.

> **Equipment:** A pack of playing cards
> **Rating:** Another piece of cake
> **Level of Difficulty:** Easy

Setup

First, deal a tableau containing six rows of six face-up cards each, forming six columns of overlapping cards. Remove any aces as they appear while you're dealing, and place them all together in a foundation row at the top.

Playing the Game

Exposed cards at the base of a column should be used to build the foundations, ascending by suit. Alternatively, the card at the base of the column can be used to build on another column, creating descending sequences, regardless of color and suit. Where appropriate, a sequence, or a part of it, can be moved as a unit. When you have made all possible moves within the tableau, start to deal your stock of unused cards, one at a time. When a card can't be built on to a foundation or placed in sequence in a column, put it at the bottom of the first, left-hand column. Once you have moved all the cards in a column, fill the space with any exposed card or sequence.

Finishing the Game

You have won when each foundation pile is complete.

Tableau for Six by Six

EIGHT OFF

The name of this game, which resembles Six by Six, possibly comes from the eight columns that make up its reserve. The object is to build sequences of cards, in their suits, from ace to king. However, there's only a 50% chance of winning.

Equipment: A pack of playing cards
Rating: One in two chance of winning
Level of Difficulty: Easy

Setup

First, deal the cards, face up, in eight columns of six cards each. Place the final four cards along the bottom as the beginning of a reserve of eight.

Playing the Game

The aim is to move the aces from the tableau to create foundations that are then built up by suit. Exposed cards at the bottom of each column and the cards in the reserve can be moved on to the foundation or placed on cards at the bottom of the columns by suit in a descending sequence. Once an exposed card has been played, the next card above it becomes available. A card can be moved into the reserve at any time but the reserve cannot exceed more than eight cards at a time. If a column becomes empty once all the cards have been moved, you can fill it with any card of any suit or rank.

Finishing the Game

The game is won when the foundations are complete.

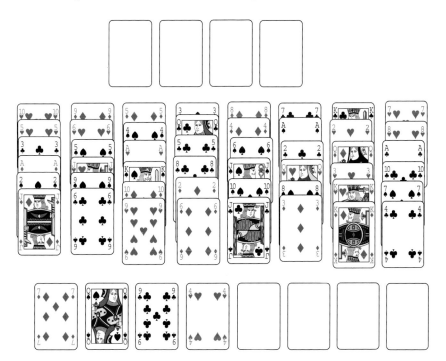

Tableau for Eight Off

HAND

Hand is a good game for playing on a journey where there's not too much room to move about. You win the game once you have removed all the cards from your hand.

Equipment: A pack of playing cards
Rating: Great for a bit of fast fun
Level of Difficulty: Easy

How to Play

Hold the deck face down in your hand. Take four cards, one at a time, from the back of the pack. Flip each one over. If the first and last belong to the same suit, remove the second and third cards. If the first and last have the same number, remove all four cards. If neither of these apply, cover the first card with the second, and flip over a new card from the back of the pack. Again, if the first and last cards belong to the same suit or have the same number, remove as previously instructed. Keep going until all cards have been removed and your hand is empty.

First and last cards are the same suit: discard second and third cards

First and last cards have the same rank: discard all four cards

DECADE

Decade is a single-pack game of solitaire in which arithmetic as well as card-playing expertise are required. A similar game, but without the arithmetic, is Accordion (see page 20).

Equipment: A pack of playing cards
Rating: Fun with figures
Level of Difficulty: Easy

How to Play

Deal the cards one at a time and place them face up next to each other. Watch the numbers or values of the cards carefully and when you find any two or more adjacent cards that add up to 10, 20 or 30, discard them. The jack, queen and king are all valued at 10 points, but cannot be discarded on their own. Aces can be high or low.

Finishing the Game

Once you have finished the stock the game ends. You have won if you have managed to discard all the cards.

EASY GO

Easy Go is a single-pack game of Patience in which you construct ascending ace-to-king suit sequences.

Equipment: A pack of playing cards
Rating: Good chance of winning
Level of Difficulty: Easy

Setup

Deal 12 face-up cards as a tableau (see illustration). Arrange the four aces above the tableau, as foundations. Use cards in the tableau to build on the foundations, building upward by suit, or place cards on each other in descending sequences, by suit. Move one card at a time.

Playing the Game

Deal one card at a time from your stock and put cards that don't fit into the foundation or tableau into a waste pile, face up. The top card of the waste pile can be used at any time. Fill spaces in the tableau with the top card of the waste pile or from your stock if there is no waste pile.

Finishing the Game

You can deal only once. The game is won when each foundation pile is complete.

Tableau for Easy Go

ACCORDION

In Accordion, there is no initial tableau. In this single-pack game, you sort the cards so that you finish with all of them where they began – in a single stack. The aim is to pile all the cards together like an accordion. However, it is seldom so straightforward.

Equipment: A pack of playing cards
Rating: Chance governs the outcome
Level of Difficulty: Easy

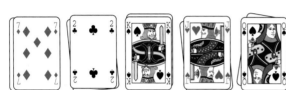

Playing Accordion

Setup

Deal five cards, face up, in a row.

Playing the Game

If a card is the same rank or the same suit as the card on its immediate left you can place it on top of that card. If it is the same rank or suit as the card three places to the left (that is, with two cards separating) place it on top of that card. If there is a choice then you must decide which you'd rather do. If the card that you are moving is the top of a pile, you move the whole pile with it.

When you've done as many moves as you can, close the gaps between the piles and deal a new card on the right. Start to make more moves, if possible. If not, deal another new card to the right. Look for more new moves.

Finishing the Game

Continue in this way until you have used all the stock cards. The game is finished when all 52 cards are piled one on top of one another.

Tip

In the illustration, you can see that the next card to be placed on a pile is the king of hearts. So, the next move could be to place the king of hearts onto the pile topped by the king of spades because they are of the same rank. A jack of hearts is already on top of the fourth pile, so, in the move after that, you can place the pile topped by the jack of hearts onto the king of hearts' pile to its left, as they are of the same suit.

ST HELENA

St Helena, a double-pack game, is named after the island where Napoleon was exiled in 1815. You build descending king-to-ace suit sequences and ascending ace-to-king suit sequences. Don't shuffle the two packs together but use them one after the other.

Equipment: Two packs of playing cards
Rating: There's scope for ingenuity here
Level of Difficulty: Easy

Setup

The rows of kings and aces shown in the illustration are the foundation cards. Deal 12 cards, clockwise, from the space above the first king, then repeat until the stock is used up.

Playing the Game

The aim is to build on the foundations, descending from king to ace and ascending from ace to king, by suit. The top four piles (numbers 1-4) are to be used for the kings only, the bottom four (7-10) for the aces, and the two side piles (5 and 6, and 11 and 12) are for both.

Use the top card of each pile to build on the foundations. You can also move the top card of a pile to create an ascending or descending suit sequence on another pile, thus exposing more cards. Fill spaces that appear with any card from any pile.

After making all feasible moves, pick up the piles backwards, from number 12 to number 1, face down, one upon the other. Without shuffling, re-deal the cards as previously. You are now free of restrictions and can build on any foundations with cards from any waste pile.

Finishing the Game

Two re-deals are allowed. The game is won when each of the foundation piles are complete.

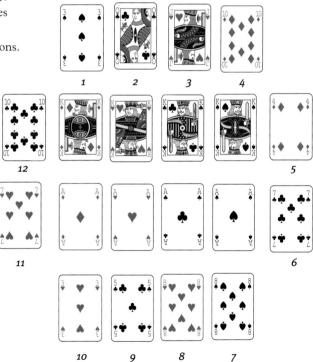

Tableau for St Helena

GRANDFATHER'S CLOCK

You don't need any particular skill to play Grandfather's Clock, and the game normally lasts between five and 10 minutes. You build a sequence of cards of the same suit, in ascending face values from deuce (two) to king, using a clock-face foundation.

> **Equipment:** A pack of playing cards
> **Rating:** Short, but sweet
> **Level of Difficulty:** Easy

Setup

Remove 12 cards: the deuce, six, and ten of clubs, the five, nine, and king of spades, the four, eight, and queen of hearts and the three, seven, and jack of diamonds. Arrange the cards in a clock-face foundation in the order illustrated.

Shuffle the remaining cards and make the tableau by arranging the rest of the cards below the clock face in eight columns of five cards each.

Playing the Game

The aim is to build on the clock-face foundations, by suit, in round-the-corner ascending sequences (so, ace on a king), until the value on the card reflects the number on a clock face. Cards from the bottom row of the tableau (the exposed cards) can be used to add to the foundation cards. You can also move exposed cards on to other exposed cards in the tableau, building in descending sequences regardless of suit. If all the cards in a column have been used, any card from the bottom row of the columns can be used to replace it.

Finishing the Game

As play progresses, piles of cards form on the clock face and a successful game is completed when the top cards in each pile read clockwise like this: ace at one o'clock, deuce at two o'clock, three at three o'clock and so on round to the queen at twelve o'clock. Sometimes, though, the cards remaining on the tableau won't allow more moves and the game ends there.

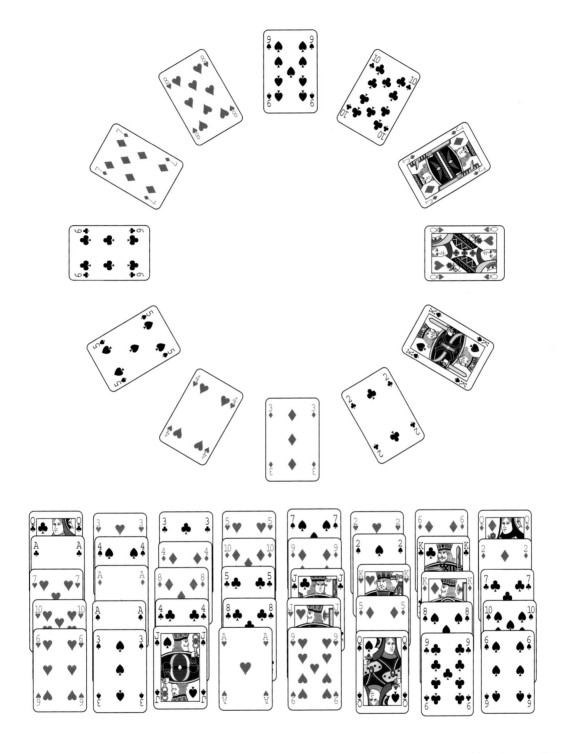

Tableau for Grandfather's Clock

MONTE CARLO

Monte Carlo, also known as Double or Quits and Weddings, is a game of chance that is played with the standard 52-card pack. The purpose of the game is to arrange the pack in 26 pairs of cards, each pair being of the same rank.

Equipment: A pack of playing cards
Rating: Undemanding fun
Level of Difficulty: Easy

Setup

Deal from left to right five rows of five cards, each face up. This is your tableau. Survey the tableau to find adjacent pairs of cards of the same rank, of any suit. These pairs of cards can be next to each other horizontally, vertically or diagonally.

Playing the Game

Take out all the adjoining pairs from the tableau and put them to one side. To fill the gaps, move the cards to the left and up (that is, move the cards in the top row to the left, then the card on the extreme left of the row below moves up to fill the space on the extreme right of the row above, and so on). Fill the gaps, now at the bottom right of the tableau, from the stock.

Finishing the Game

Repeat the process above, removing adjoining pairs and filling the space left. Continue the same way until you have 26 pairs of cards put aside in a pile. This means you have won the game.

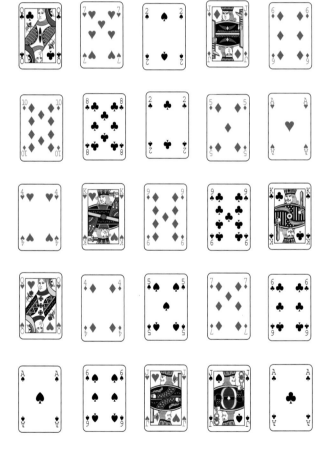

Tableau for Monte Carlo

BLOCK ELEVEN

Also known as Calling Out, Block Eleven is a short but intense game that lasts around two minutes. Once you have dealt the tableau, one of the picture or face cards must be at the bottom of the pack if you're going to have a chance of winning the game.

> **Equipment:** A pack of playing cards
> **Rating:** Good for occupying a couple of minutes
> **Level of Difficulty:** Easy

Setup

Lay out 12 number cards in three rows of four cards each. Shuffle the other 40 cards, making sure that one of the picture cards is at the bottom of the pack.

Playing the Game

Now survey your tableau to find any two cards whose numbers add up to 11 (aces are low.) Place a card dealt from your stock on each of them, then survey your tableau again, looking for two other cards whose numbers add up to 11. Continue like this until a picture card lies on top of one of the piles. Once this happens, you can't add any more cards to that pile.

Finishing the Game

Choose another two cards adding up to 11 and deal more cards until another picture card comes to the top. You have won the game when you have dealt all 40 cards into piles and there are picture cards at the top of them all.

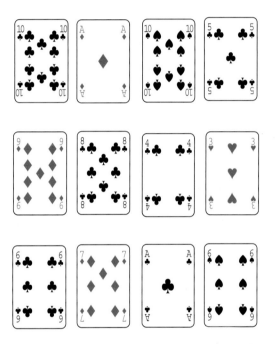

Tableau for Block Eleven

FLORENTINE

In this single-pack game, the ace or king doesn't always act as a foundation for the sequence piles. Foundation cards are chosen by the way you deal the cards at the start. The purpose of Florentine is to build round-the-corner ascending suit sequences.

Equipment: A pack of playing cards
Rating: A nice, no-frills game
Level of Difficulty: Easy

Setup

Deal a tableau of five face-up cards in a cross-shape (see illustration). Next, deal a separate sixth card as the first of four foundations. Note the rank of this sixth card, because the other three foundations must be of the same rank.

Playing the Game

The aim is to build on the foundation cards, ascending by suit. However, you can also build on the four outer cards of the cross, descending, by number (so, any suit or color). Cards can be moved from the cross to the foundation piles or to another pile in the cross. The middle card cannot be built on, but can be moved to a foundation pile.

Deal cards one at a time. Add any further foundation cards (in this case, cards with the number seven) to the foundation row. Those cards that can't contribute to a sequence go to a waste pile, face up. Any resulting spaces in the cross can be filled by the top card of the waste pile or the middle card of the cross, in which case you should replace the middle card of the cross with the top card of the waste pile.

Finishing the Game

When you've made all possible moves, turn the waste pile over and re-deal without shuffling it first. You can only re-deal once. The game is finished when each foundation pile contains 13 cards.

Tableau for Florentine

COLORADO

In the double-pack game of Colorado, you build two kinds of same-suit sequences, ace ascending to king and king descending to ace.

> **Equipment:** Two packs of playing cards
> **Rating:** Win five out of six games
> **Level of Difficulty:** Easy

Setup

Deal two rows of 10 cards, face up, as your tableau.

Playing the Game

Search the tableau for aces and kings and move to a row above as foundation cards. Again, search the tableau and put eligible cards on foundation cards, building sequences upward by suit from ace to king and downward by suit from king to ace. Replace any holes in the tableau with cards from the stock. Deal the cards one at a time, looking out for foundation cards and cards that can be built on foundations.

If a card cannot be used, it can be place on any tableau card, as on a waste pile, regardless of suit or value. You can't move a card from one of the tableau piles to another or deal a fresh card from stock until you have found a place for the previous stock card. On each deal, continue to move dealt cards and tableau cards to foundation piles.

Finishing the Game

The game is finished after the stock has run out, the tableau is empty and all the foundation suit sequences are complete.

Tableau for Colorado

GATE

This solitaire game takes its name from the shape formed by its reserve, its tableau and its ace foundations, which together make it resemble a triple-barred gate.

Equipment: A pack of playing cards
Rating: Straightforward, uncomplicated game
Level of Difficulty: Easy

Setup

Deal two columns of five cards each, face up, with four cards' space between the columns. These columns form the reserve, known as the gateposts. Then deal two rows of four cards between the gateposts – these are known as the rails.

Playing the Game

The object of the game is to build up ace-to-king sequences by suit on the four ace foundations. Deal the stock one card at a time to a waste pile. As the aces appear, place them in a row above the top rail of the gate to form the foundations. Once you have a foundation, you can begin to build sequences, using cards from the stock or from the rails. Fill gaps in the rails with cards from the stock, or from the gateposts, until there are no gatepost cards left. The top card of the waste pile is always available for play.

You can place cards from the tableau rows on other cards in the tableau, in descending sequence, but these must alternate in color.

Finishing the game

Keep dealing until your stock of cards runs out. There are no redeals in Gate. You have won the game if you have built four suit sequences on the foundations.

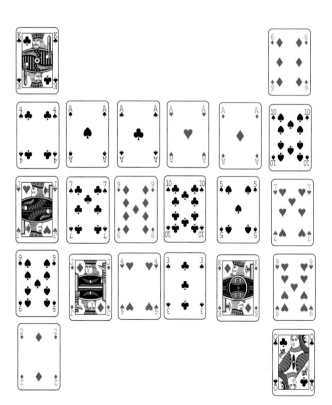

Tableau and Foundations for Gate

HALF MOON

This game takes its title from the semicircle formed by 12 packets of eight cards each. The aim is to remove any two face-up cards from the pack whose numbers total 11, and any sequences of any suit of jack, queen and king turned face up together.

> **Equipment:** Two packs of playing cards
> **Rating:** How's your mental arithmetic?
> **Level of Difficulty:** Easy

Tableau for Half Moon

Setup

Shuffle the cards. Start by dealing eight cards, face up, in a row to use as your reserve. Above the reserve deal the remaining 96 cards, face down, in a half moon shape, consisting of 12 packets (piles) of eight cards each. Turn the top card of each packet face up.

Playing the Game

Survey the cards at the top of the packets and remove any two exposed cards that add up to 11, and any sequences of jack, queen and king, of any suit, which are exposed together (not necessarily next to each other), and put them aside. Where you've removed cards from the top of a packet, turn the card underneath face up. This makes it available to

be played. Continue in this way. Use the cards from the reserve if you have to, but not if a card of the same rank is available on a packet. Cards should not be moved into any empty spaces that arise, either in the half moon or in the tableau.

A situation may arise where two or more cards of the same rank have risen to the top of a packet. If this happens, you are allowed to take a look at the cards underneath this inconvenient pair so that you can choose which of the top cards would be best to play.

Finishing the Game

You have won the game when you end up with all the cards removed from both the half moon and the reserve.

ACES UP

This game has many different names. It's also called Easthaven, Idiot's Delight, Once in a Lifetime, ace of the Pile, and Firing Squad. The aim is to finish with all of the cards discarded and all the aces in the tableau. The chances of winning are only around one in 30.

> **Equipment:** A pack of playing cards
> **Rating:** One in 30 chance to win
> **Level of Difficulty:** Easy

Setup

First, deal four cards, face up, in a tableau.

Playing the Game

Look at the tableau and try to find two or more cards of the same suit, and discard the lowest card and leave the highest. If three or four cards are of the same suit, discard all of them except the highest one. Remember that an ace ranks higher than a king, so if you find both of them, keep the ace and discard the king. Deal new cards into the holes left by the discarded cards.

If all the cards are of different suits, then deal another four cards on top and continue. If one of the tableau piles becomes empty, start a new pile with the top card of any of the other three piles. Continue until the stock runs out.

Finishing the Game

If, at the end of the game, all four aces remain in the tableau, and all the others are discarded, then you have won.

Tableau for Aces Up

BELVEDERE

In Belvedere, the tableau consists of fans of cards, foundations, and a reserve. The game is not as complicated as it looks, and lots more fun.

> **Equipment:** A pack of playing cards
> **Rating:** A fun game with a pleasing tableau
> **Level of Difficulty:** Easy

Setup

Place any one of the aces down as the first foundation card. Then, deal 24 cards from the pack, face up, in eight fans of three cards each. Any kings you have dealt should be moved to make it the first card on the left of its fan. As you deal them, the other three aces should be placed in a foundation row. Finally, place three cards in a row below the fan layout, as your reserve.

Playing the Game

The aim is to build upward on the foundation cards, by suit. To build your sequences, the exposed card on the right of each fan and the top card of a reserve pile can be placed on a foundation. The exposed cards of the fans can be placed on one another in descending sequences, regardless of suit or colour. The cards in the reserve can be placed on the fans. Only move one card at a time.

Spaces in the layout caused when all the cards in a fan have been moved should not be filled.

Finishing the Game

Once you have made all the moves open to you, deal your stock three at a time, on top of the three reserve cards (or gaps therein) and continue. Once you have dealt all the cards in your stock, the game is finished. You have won if you have four complete ace-to-king ascending piles.

Tableau for Belvedere

PERPETUAL MOTION

Perpetual Motion is sometimes known as Idiot's Delight. It only uses a single pack, but takes quite a lot of time, because you need to deal several times before the object of the game – to remove all the cards in the tableau piles – is achieved.

Equipment: A pack of cards
Rating: Time consuming
Level of Difficulty: Easy

Playing Perpetual Motion: Deal one

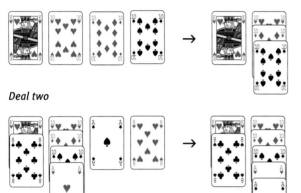

Deal two

Deal three

Deal four

No cards can be moved leftward from Deal Four, so proceed by dealing four more cards as before.

Setup

Start by dealing one card to each of four piles. Keep the rest of the pack as your stock. If you find you have dealt two or three cards of the same rank, pile the cards in an overlapping column on the card furthest to the left (see illustration: the three tens have been piled on the ten furthest to the left). If you deal four cards of the same rank, you should discard those four cards.

Playing the Game

Now deal another four cards on top of the first four in the tableau, or any gaps therein, creating columns of overlapping cards. Only the top card (the exposed card) of each column is in play now. Move any duplicates in the same way, in a leftwards direction.

Keep on dealing, moving cards and, where appropriate, discarding until you reach the end of the pack.

Starting at the right, pick up each pile and place them one over the other, either face down or face up. Don't mix up the order of the cards in their piles. Deal another four cards, and start again in the same way as before. You can deal as many times as you like.

Finishing the Game

The game has finished and you have won when the stock is used up and all cards are discarded in groups of four.

CRUEL

Cruel, which is similar to Perseverance (see page 70) is played with a single pack. The aim is to create a sequence of cards on the foundations, ascending from ace to king, by suit.

> **Equipment:** A pack of playing cards
> **Rating:** You'll always win if you play long enough
> **Level of Difficulty:** Easy

Setup

Start by removing all four aces from the pack. Place them in a row to serve as foundations for the game. Next, put the other 48 cards into a tableau comprising 12 piles of four cards each, face up.

Playing the Game

The top card of each pile is the only one available for play at any one time. Use these cards to build on the foundation piles, building the sequences up from ace to king, by suit. You can also use them to build on the tableau piles in a dscending sequence from king to ace, by suit. Gaps in the tableau are not filled at this stage.

If you find you cannot make any more moves, put the remaining piles one on top of the other face up, starting with the last pile you dealt, and proceeding to the first. Deal the cards again into piles of four each. You may do this as many times as you like and you can, in fact, keep going until you have won the game.

Finishing the Game

You have won the game when you have created a sequence of cards on the foundations, ascending from ace to king, by suit.

Tableau for Cruel

DEUCES

Deuces is a double-deck game that gets its name from the deuces, or twos, that start each of the foundations.

> **Equipment:** Two packs of playing cards
> **Rating:** Keep your wits about you
> **Level of Difficulty:** Moderate

Setup

Take the eight deuce (two) cards out of the packs. Set them in two rows of four each to form the foundations. Next, deal ten cards and place four above the deuce foundation rows, three to the left of the foundations and another three to the right, all face up.

Object of the Game

The object is to build foundation piles by suit from the deuces up to aces.

Playing the Game

Deal one card at a time from your stock and, as suitable cards become available, place them on the appropriate foundations. You can also build sequences within the tableau, by suit, in descending order.
You are allowed to build kings on aces in the tableau. Use the top cards of the tableau piles to place on the foundations or other tableau piles. You can move entire or part-sequences as a unit. Cards that can't take part in building the sequences should be placed on a waste pile, face up, and the top card can be used at any time if it contributes to a sequence. Spaces in the tableau caused by moving cards should be filled by dealing from the waste pile. There are no redeals in Deuces.

Finishing the Game

You are finished and have won when all the foundation piles have aces on top.

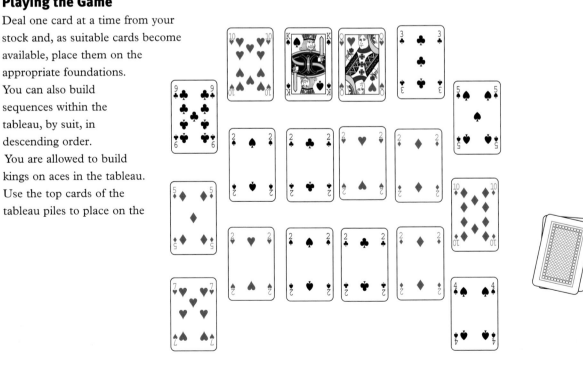

Tableau for Deuces

STONEWALL

Stonewall is a one-pack game and the object is to make the aces the foundations for ascending same-suit sequences. In order to do this, you have to break down the walls of cards.

Equipment: A pack of playing cards
Rating: You need a good run of cards to win
Level of Difficulty: Moderate

Setup

Lay out the tableau by dealing 36 cards into six columns of six cards each. This tableau has a distinctive pattern (see illustration above). The second, fourth and sixth rows are face up and the first, third and fifth are face down. You will have 16 cards left over to act as your reserve; fan these below the tableau, face up.

Object of the Game

The aim is to find the aces to create foundations, then build on these, ascending by suit, ace to king.

Playing the Game

The exposed cards at the bottom of each column and the reserve cards are open to play and can be used to build on a foundation. These can also be used to build on the exposed cards, in a descending sequence by alternating colours. If an exposed card is removed, leaving a downward facing card, turn this card over to become the new exposed card. You are allowed to move a sequence of cards as a single unit. Fill empty columns using an exposed card or sequence.

Finishing the Game

The game is complete when no more moves can be made, and won when all four foundation piles are complete with kings at the top of each.

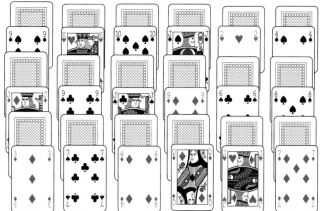

Tableau for Stonewall

WESTCLIFF

In Westcliff, which uses a single pack of cards, the aim is to build ascending ace-to-king sequences in suits. Westcliff is challenging, but you can probably win 80 or 90 percent of the time.

> **Equipment:** A pack of playing cards
> **Rating:** Good chance to win
> **Level of Difficulty:** Moderate

Setup
First, deal a tableau of 30 cards in ten rows of three cards each (see illustration). As they appear, place the aces in a foundation row just above the tableau.

Object of the Game
The aim is to build ascending ace-to-king sequences in suits, on the four aces.

Playing the Game
Where you can, place face-up cards directly on the foundation cards or on other face-up cards, descending by

alternate colors. Sequences of cards can be moved to other columns if applicable. When a face-down card reaches the bottom of a column, turn it face up and use it for building sequences. When all moves are made, deal the stock cards one at a time and look for more moves. Any card that doesn't fit in to the foundations or the columns in the tableau goes to a waste pile, face up. The top card of the pile is always available for building a sequence if it is suitable. You can use a card from the waste pile to replace an empty column after all its cards have been moved.

Finishing the Game
The stock cards can only be dealt once. The game is over when you can no longer move and you have won when all the cards are arranged on the foundation piles.

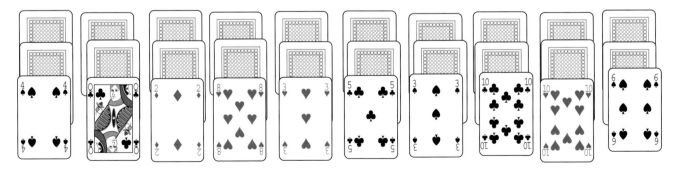

Tableau for Westcliff

36

RED AND BLACK

Red and Black takes its name from the alternating colours used for building sequences. A two-pack game, it has no relation to Rouge et Noir, even though it translates, confusingly, as Red and Black.

Equipment: Two packs of playing cards
Rating: Needs concentration
Level of Difficulty: Moderate

Setup

Remove the eight aces from the double pack and lay them down in a foundation row. Underneath, deal eight cards to create a tableau.

Object of the Game

The aim is to build up the foundation cards, by suit, ace to king.

Playing the Game

Cards in the tableau can be moved to build on a foundation. They can also be moved to build on another tableau card in descending order, in alternating colours. When all moves

have been made, deal the stock, one card at a time, and place on a foundation or tableau card. Any cards that cannot be used should be placed face up on a waste pile. The top card of the waste pile is available to use at any time. Fill spaces with cards from the waste pile, or stock if there is no waste pile. Any sequences built in the tableau can be moved as a unit.

Finishing the Game

When you have no more stock cards, the game is finished. There is only one deal. You have won when the foundation piles are complete.

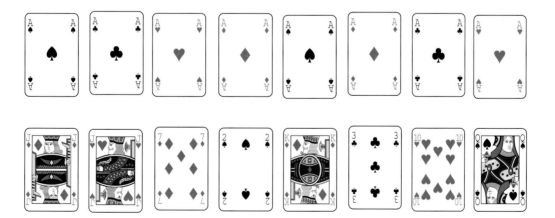

Tableau for Red and Black

BRITISH CONSTITUTION

Also known simply as Constitution, this is a two-pack game of solitaire that allows you a good chance of winning. The aim of the game is to finish with all the cards built on to the foundations with the jacks at the top.

> **Equipment:** Two packs of playing cards, without kings or queens
> **Rating:** You have a good chance of winning
> **Level of Difficulty:** Moderate

Setup

In this game the foundation row is called the 'Government', the tableau is the 'Constitution', and the cards used for building on the foundations are the 'Privy Council'. The kings and queens are taken out of the pack and play no part. Take out all eight aces from the pack and place them in a row to form the foundations. Deal a tableau of four rows of eight cards below the aces, face up. The remaining cards form your stock.

Object of the Game

The aim is to build eight foundations on the aces in ascending sequence (two to jack) by suit.

Playing the Game

From the top row of the tableau only, place suitable cards on the foundations. Descending sequences can also be built on the top row using cards from this row or from the second row. Cards can only be moved one at a time, and spaces left should be filled with the card from the row immediately below. This, in turn, leaves a space in the second or third row, which is filled from the third or fourth row. When the space reaches the fourth row, fill the gap with a card from the stock. Note that stock cards cannot enter the game anywhere other than the bottom row, and cannot be played directly to the foundations.

Finishing the Game

You have won when all the cards are built on to the foundations from ace to jack.

Tableau for British Constitution

CRESCENT

Crescent gets its name from its semicircular tableau. The aim is to move all the cards from the crescent to the foundations, where you build ascending ace-to-king suit sequences and descending king-to-ace suit sequences.

Equipment: Two packs of playing cards
Rating: Unusual tableau makes for extra interest
Level of Difficulty: Moderate

Setup

Remove one king and one ace from each of the four suits to form bases for the foundations. Place the kings in a row, with the aces below them. Next, in a semicircle, deal 16 piles each of six face-down cards.

Object of the Game

The aim is to build ascending (ace to king) sequences on the aces and descending (king to ace) sequences on the kings, by suit, going round-the-corner where necessary (that is, place a king over an ace or vice versa).

Playing the Game

Turn over one card at a time from the top of a pile in the crescent. If the card cannot be used, it must remain on top of its pile, face up, and can be used at any later part of the game. An empty space in the tableau cannot be filled. As the game progresses, you can transfer cards, except for the kings and aces at the base, from one foundation to another.

Finishing the Game

Once all possible moves have been made, you may continue the game with a special re-deal. Remove the bottom card of each pile in the crescent and place it on the top, face up. You can do this only three times per game. You have won the game when all cards are in suit sequence on the foundations.

A game of Crescent in progress

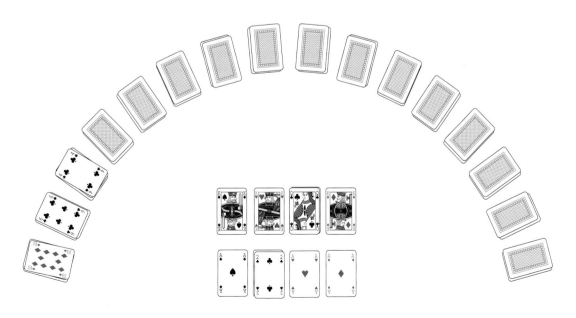

DUCHESS

The single-pack game of solitaire known as Duchess affords a good chance of winning. But in Duchess, the sequences aren't necessarily the usual ace-to-king, king-to-ace pattern.

Equipment: A pack of playing cards
Rating: Very good chance to win
Level of Difficulty: Moderate

Tableau for Duchess

Setup

Deal four fans of three cards each to act as the reserve. Leave a space for four foundation cards, then place another four cards in a row as bases for the tableau columns. Choose an exposed card (on the right of a fan) from the reserve to begin the first foundation pile. The choice is yours, but the chosen card must be followed by three others of the same rank. As you find them, put them in place.

Object of the Game

The object of the game is to build up the four foundations by suit, in round-the-corner fashion (i.e. kings can be placed on aces).

Playing the Game

Move the exposed cards of the reserve and tableau columns to build the sequences. On the tableau, cards are built downwards in alternating colours. When all moves have been made, turn over the stock cards one at a time and move to the foundation or tableau. Cards that don't qualify go to a waste pile, face up, the top card of which can always be used, if appropriate. As spaces appear in the tableau, fill them with any top card in the reserve. Fill spaces in the reserve with cards from the waste pile. If there is no waste pile, use cards from your stock.

Finishing the Game

You are allowed one re-deal in Duchess, using cards from the waste pile turned face down. The game finishes when all the foundation piles are complete.

CARPET

In Carpet, once you deal 20 cards for the tableau (the carpet of the game's title), you can't place any more cards on them. This makes things tricky! You can place cards only on the four aces that are dealt in a row above the tableau that form the foundations.

> **Equipment:** A pack of playing cards
> **Rating:** Straightforward and easy to win
> **Level of Difficulty:** Moderate

Setup
Take the four aces out of the pack and place them in a row. Below the aces, deal a 'carpet' of 20 cards in four rows of five each.

Object of the Game
The object of the game is to build ace-to-king sequences by suit.

Playing the Game
All the cards in the carpet are available for placing on the ace foundations, as long as they help form the ascending-suit sequences. Deal from the stock, one at a time, and try to place on the foundations. If this is impossible, put them in a waste pile, face up.

Finishing the Game
Fill spaces that are left in the carpet with cards from the waste pile. If there is no waste pile, then fill the space from your stock of unused cards. You can deal the card stock only once and when that runs out, that's the end of the game. You have won if the foundation piles are complete.

Tableau for Carpet

SALIC LAW

This double-pack game of solitaire is named after a
French law of 1316 barring women and their male
descendants from the throne. Here, this is symbolized
by discarding the eight queens at the start of the
game and playing without them.

> **Equipment:** Two packs of playing cards with queens removed
> **Rating:** Needs skill and judgment
> **Level of Difficulty:** Moderate

Setup

Remove all queens from the packs of cards. First, remove an
ace from the pack and place it on your left-hand side to start
your tableau. Next, take any one king from the pack and
place it beneath the ace. Using the first king as a base, deal
overlapping cards until you find the next king. Place it to the
right of the first and deal a column of further overlapping
cards until you uncover the third king. Carry on until you
have eight columns. As you find aces, put them on the
foundation row. If, as you deal, you find other cards suitable
for building on foundations, you can move them directly.

Object of the Game

The object of the game is to build ascending ace-to-jack
sequences by numerical value alone, not by suit or color.

Playing the Game

Once you have dealt the tableau, use the cards at the base of
each column to build on the foundations. Sequences cannot
be built on the tableau cards. However, if a column consists
of a single king, any exposed card can be placed in this
column.

Finishing the Game

You win the game when the foundations contain all the
available cards.

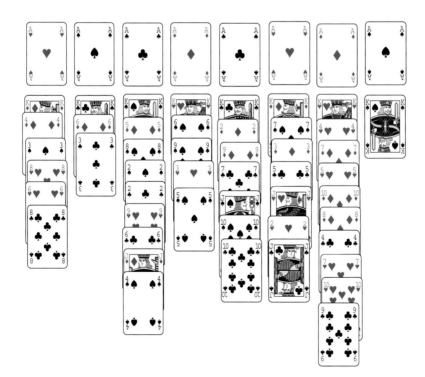

Tableau for Salic Law

PARISIAN

Parisian, also called Parisienne, is a variation on Grand Duchess (see page 54). It is a two-pack game in which you build ascending ace-to-king and descending king-to-ace suit sequences.

> **Equipment:** Two packs of playing cards
> **Rating:** Plenty of scope to complete the game
> **Level of Difficulty:** Moderate

Setup

Find four aces and four kings of each suit and line them up in two rows as the foundations. Create a small tableau of one row of 4 cards dealt face up, as shown in the illustration, and put two cards aside, face down.

Object of the Game

The object of the game is to build ascending ace-to-king sequences on the aces and descending king-to-ace sequences on the kings.

Playing the Game

Build on the foundations using the face-up cards in the tableau. When you can't build further with the cards available, deal four more cards from your stock, placing them on top of the original four (or their empty spaces) and also, put aside two cards, face down. Keep going in the same way until your stock runs out.

Now gather up all the cards in the face down piles, look at all of them, and use suitable cards in any order to build on the foundations. Then check to see if you can build further using the exposed tableau cards.

When no further moves are possible, gather up all the tableau piles and shuffle them. Put the remaining reserve pile at the bottom of the pack, and redeal the four-card tableau as before. Four such deals are allowed. In the fourth and final deal, all the cards are dealt to the tableau and none are kept aside for the reserve.

Finishing the Game

You have won if you end up with eight completed foundation piles.

Foundation rows for Parisian

Tableau for Parisian

MOUNT OLYMPUS

**In Mount Olympus, the object is to build suit sequences, ascending from the aces and the Deuces (twos).
The game is unusual as you have to build the odd-numbered cards on the ace (A, 3, 5, 7, 9, J, K) and the even-numbered cards on the Deuces (2, 4, 6, 8, 10, Q).**

Equipment: Two packs of playing cards
Rating: Needs concentration
Level of Difficulty: Moderate

Setup

Remove the aces and the deuces from the packs and lay them out as foundation rows. Below them, deal a tableau of nine face-up cards, as shown in the diagram.

Object of the Game

Your aim is to build ascending suit sequences, using odd-numbered cards on the aces and even-numbered cards on the deuces.

Playing the Game

Build sequences on the foundations using the cards in the tableau. You can place cards in the tableau on each other, in

descending sequences by twos. A sequence of cards can be moved as one unit. Fill any spaces in the tableau from your stock of cards.

Finishing the Game

Once you have made all possible moves, deal a row of nine cards on top of the cards in the tableau, face up. Continue playing from the tableau to the foundations for as long as you can. Ideally, you will end up with all the suit sequences in correct order, in which case you have won.

Tableau and foundations for Mount Olympus

SHAMROCKS

Shamrocks gets its name from the groups of three cards in the tableau, which resemble the leaves of a shamrock. It is a similar game to Lovely Lucy (see page 61).

> **Equipment:** A pack of playing cards
> **Rating:** Follow the rules with care
> **Level of Difficulty:** Moderate

Setup

Deal three cards at a time into 17 'shamrocks'. The last, fifty-second, card is placed in the tableau on its own, as an incomplete fan.

Object of the Game

The aim is to build ascending sequences on the foundation aces, by suit.

Playing of the Game

Only the exposed top card of each fan is available for play. Use any exposed ace to begin the foundations, then start to build on the foundations by suit. You can move an exposed card to another pile on the tableau and build up or down in sequence, regardless of suit. However, you can't have more than three cards on a fan at one time, so a fan that already contains three cards can't acquire any additions. An empty fan cannot be replaced.

Finishing the Game

Wins are rare and you need to have kings as the bottom card on at least one of your fans. You have won when all the foundation piles are complete.

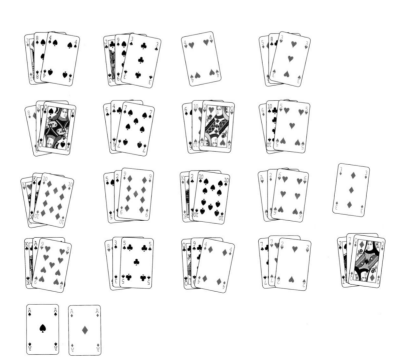

Playing Shamrocks

EAGLE WINGS

This game takes its name from the shape of the card arrangement. The aim is to build same-suit sequences of cards that run round-the-corner: the highest card sits next to the lowest, and a sequence running to a king goes round-the-corner to an ace.

Equipment: A pack of playing cards
Rating: Winning depends on how the cards are dealt
Level of Difficulty: Moderate

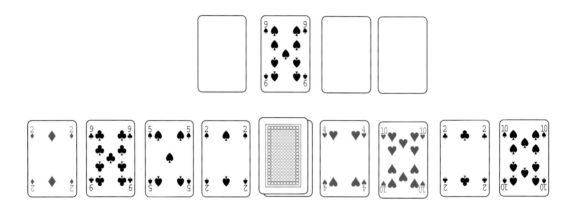

Tableau for Eagle Wings

Setup

Create the 'heel' by dealing a pile of 13 face-down cards. Next, make the 'wings' with four cards in a row on either side of the heel. Place another card, face up, above the heel as the first foundation. As the game proceeds and three other cards of the same rank as the first foundation card appear, place them in the same row above the heel.

Object of the Game

The aim is to build the foundations in descending order by suit.

Use the eight wing cards to build the foundations. As gaps arise in the wings, fill them with cards from the heel, turned face up. When no more moves can be made from the wings, deal a card from the stock pile. Cards that can't be placed on a foundation go to the waste pile, face up, where the top card can be played at any time. The last remaining card in the heel pile can be turned face up and played directly to the foundation (it doesn't need to wait for a space on the wing). Any space on the wing can now be filled with cards from the waste pile or stock.

Finishing the Game

Keep the game going by dealing cards from the stock. You can re-deal three times, but you mustn't shuffle the cards. The game has been won if, at the end of the fourth deal, there is a complete set of cards on each foundation.

AMAZONS

Amazons takes its name from the legendary race of female warriors. This is because in this game, kings play no part, and (if you win) the queens should always come out on top!

> **Equipment:** A pack of playing cards with twos through sixes and kings removed
> **Rating:** This one's unusual
> **Level of Difficulty:** Moderate

Setup

After stripping the pack (see above), deal four cards as your reserve. The aces that will form the foundations should be placed above the reserve, as they appear.

Object of the Game

The aim is to build sequences of ace, seven, eight, nine, ten, jack, queen on the four foundations.

Playing the Game

Move eligible cards from the reserve to the foundations. All cards (except foundation aces) can only be moved to the pile directly above, except for the queen, which can move to any foundation from any reserve pile.

When all possible moves have been made, deal another four cards, one on each reserve pile and check to see if you can put more cards on the foundations. Continue dealing and building sequences until your stock of cards runs out. Make a new stock by putting each pile over the pile to its right, and turning them face down. Don't re-shuffle the cards before you re-deal them and start again with a reserve of four cards.

Finishing the Game

You can re-deal as many times as you like. If you go on long enough to win the game, you should have all the cards on the foundations, with the queens at the top.

Tableau for Amazons

BLACK HOLE

Black Hole takes its name from an astronomical phenomenon in which the collapse of a massive star creates a gravity well from which nothing can escape. Here, no card is supposed to escape. The idea is to compress the whole 52-card deck into a single foundation.

> **Equipment:** A pack of playing cards
> **Rating:** Needs concentration
> **Level of Difficulty:** Moderate

Setup

First, deal the cards so that they form a tableau of 17 piles of three. There will be one card left over and this is the Black Hole, which is placed as a lone foundation for the game. Normally, this Black Hole card is the ace of Spades, but any card can serve the same purpose.

Object of the Game

The object is to end up with all 52 cards piled on the Black Hole, in rank order, regardless of suit or color.

Playing the Game

Move the exposed cards in the piles, one at a time, to the foundation pile where they must be either one rank higher or lower than the top card already on the Black Hole, regardless of suit. As you move an exposed card, the card beneath then becomes exposed. Build round-the-corner, from ace to king or king to ace, as appropriate.

Finishing the Game

The end of the game comes when you can no longer move. You have won if you've placed all the cards on the hole.

Tableau for Black Hole

PERSIAN

Persian is a double-pack game in which you build eight ace-to-king foundation sequences. However, 40 cards are removed at the start so that the seven is the next card after the ace.

Equipment: Two packs of playing cards with twos through sixes removed
Rating: Unusual solitaire game
Level of Difficulty: Moderate

Setup

Deal the remaining 64 cards, face up, in eight overlapping rows of eight cards each. As they emerge while dealing, set the aces aside to serve as foundations.

Object of the Game

The object of the game is to build ace-to-king (i.e. ace, 7, 8, 9, 10, jack, queen, king) sequences on the foundations.

Playing the Game

Only the bottom cards of the eight columns can be built on the foundations. These exposed cards can also be placed on each other in descending sequences in alternating color. When any column is empty, you can fill it with any card

from the bottom row or with a sequence.

Once you have gone as far as you can in building on the foundations, you are allowed three more deals. Pick up the cards remaining in the tableau and shuffle them. Deal them again in eight new columns (though not all of the columns will contain eight cards). If it's not possible to move any of the cards in the first deal, that deal doesn't count and you still have three to play with.

Finishing the Game

The game is over when you have made all possible deals and moves. If you have eight complete ace-to-king sequences on the foundations, you have won.

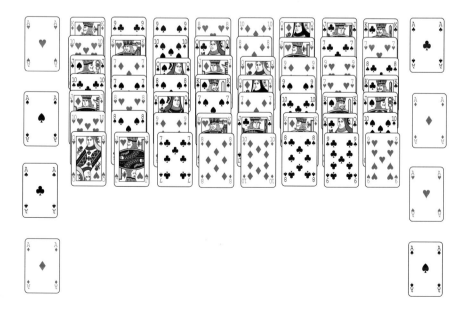

Tableau for Persian

SLY FOX

Sly Fox is a double-pack game in which there are two sets of foundations, one based on the ace and the other on the king. Unusually, cards can't be placed onto the tableau, but go directly on to one or other of the foundations.

> **Equipment:** Two packs of playinig cards
> **Rating:** Relatively easy to win
> **Level of Difficulty:** Moderate

Setup

Remove one ace and one king of each suit from the double pack. Line up the aces vertically on the far left and the kings on the far right, to create foundations, as shown in the illustration. Next, deal a tableau of five rows with four cards each between the ace and king columns.

Object of the Game

In Sly Fox, you build ascending ace-to-king suit sequences, and descending king-to-ace suit sequences.

Playing the Game

Start building sequences from the tableau. You'll find that spaces appear, and these can be filled by cards from your stock. When you have made all moves possible, and all the spaces are filled, deal 20 cards from your stock on top of the cards already in the tableau. Piles can have more than two cards or only one card.

Now, once again, you can take cards from the tableau to place on the foundations. You can no longer refill spaces. When no more moves can be made, deal another 20 cards, and continue as before.

Finishing the Game

The game ends when your stock of cards is exhausted and you have won when the foundations are complete.

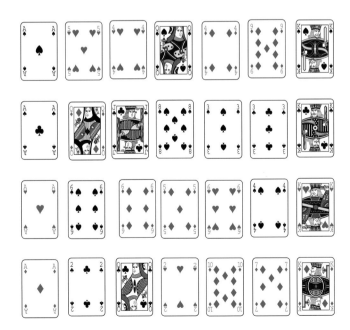

Tableau for Sly Fox

SPIDERETTE

Despite the similarity in names, Spiderette has no connection with Little Spider (see page 109). The aim is to build within the layout – not in separate foundations – four full sets of descending king-to-ace sequences, and then discard all of them!

Equipment: A pack of playing cards
Rating: Needs concentration
Level of Difficulty: Moderate

Setup
Deal a 28-card tableau, as shown.

Object of the Game
The aim is to build sequences in descending order, regardless of suit or color.

Playing the Game
Only the exposed cards in the tableau columns can be played. A group of same-suit cards can be moved as a unit. When a face-down card is exposed, turn it face up and use it for sequence building. You can fill a space in an empty column with any card or sequence you like. Once you have made all possible moves, deal another set of cards, face up, on top of each of the seven columns, and continue making moves. When you build a king-to-ace sequence, remove it from play.

Keep dealing out seven cards at a time until you have only three cards left in your stock. If you still can't get further with the sequences, place each of these cards in each of the first three columns.

Finishing the Game
The game ends if you can't make moves and you win if you have four king-to-ace sequences built and discarded.

Tableau for Spiderette

STRATEGY

Strategy is said to belong to the same solitaire family as Sir Tommy (see page 14), but it's a more difficult version. Only one pack of cards is used.

▌ Equipment: A pack of playing cards
▌ Rating: Fun to play
▌ Level of Difficulty: Moderate

Playing the Game

Deal the cards one at a time and place the aces onto foundations as they appear. There, ace-to-king sequences will be built up by suit. As the dealing progresses, place any cards that can't be placed on the foundations in eight waste piles, face up. The top cards of the waste piles can be used, where appropriate, to help build the sequences, however, you can't move cards from one waste pile to another. The game ends after you have dealt all your cards. If you have cards still on the waste piles at this point, you've lost. Winning means having all the cards on the foundations, placed in ascending suit order.

STAR

The game of Star takes its name from its star-shaped tableau (opposite). It is also known as Shah (Persian for 'king') because the king forms the central point of the star.

▌ Equipment: Two packs of playing cards without seven of the kings
▌ Rating: Unusual layout requires care
▌ Level of Difficulty: Moderate

Setup

Place one king of hearts at the middle of your playing area. The other kings play no part in the game, so remove and set them aside. Arrange the eight aces around the king as foundations, as shown opposite. Next, place one card from your stock on the outside of each ace. If you deal a deuce (two), place it on its corresponding ace foundation, and continue dealing, filling in any gaps from the stock. If a deuce has already been dealt and you find a three, set it on the appropriate foundation, and so on. Make three deals to the outside of each ace, creating a star.

Object of the Game

The aim of this game is to build ace-to-queen suit sequences surrounding the king.

Playing the Game

The outside cards of the tableau are available to play. You can build on the outside cards in descending suit sequences which can, when possible, be moved from one outside card to another. When an outside card is used, the next card becomes available for play. If all the cards on a ray have been moved, you can fill the space with a card from anywhere else in the outer circle. If no moves are possible, deal cards one by one from the stock. If they cannot be built on a foundation or used to form sequences in the rays, play them to a waste heap. The top card of the waste heap is always available for play.

Finishing the Game

The game is finished when no more moves can be made. You have won if the foundations are complete.

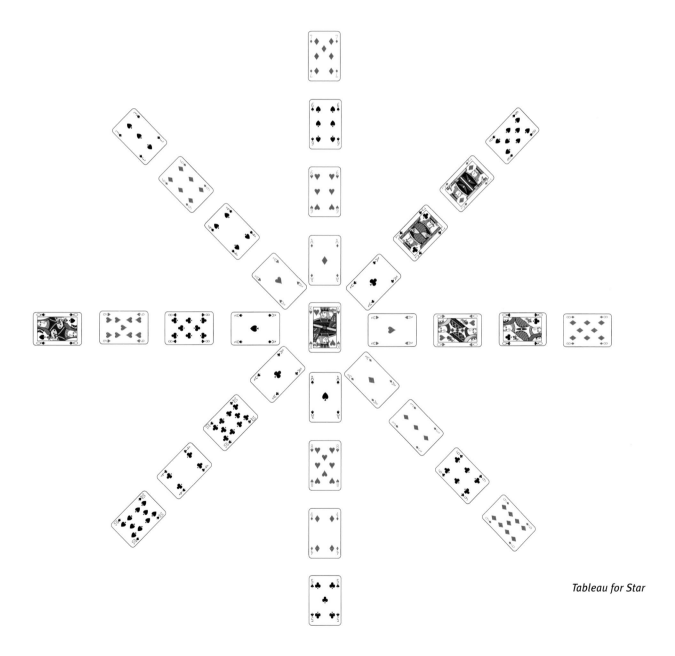

Tableau for Star

GRAND DUCHESS

Grand Duchess has an unusual reserve of cards: you don't use it until your stock has run out. In Grand Duchess , you build two sets of foundations, both sequenced by suit – one ascending ace to king, the other descending king to ace.

> **Equipment:** Two packs of playing cards
> **Rating:** Needs concentration
> **Level of Difficulty:** Moderate

Setup

Deal a row of four cards face-up and two cards face-down. These cards form the start of your four tableau piles and two reserve piles, as shown in the diagram.

Object of the Game

The object of the game is to end up with eight columns of cards, each column containing a complete suit. These are divided into two sets: one set has four columns in descending order (K, Q, J …3, 2, A), while the other set has four columns in ascending order (A, 2, 3 … J, Q, K).

A game of Grand Duchess

Playing the Game

Look at your initial tableau piles. Place any eligible top cards in a row to form the foundations (one king and one ace in each suit). Once you have moved all eligible cards, deal another six cards onto your tableau and reserves piles in the same way as you did initially (four face-up; two face-down). Put any eligible cards on the foundations as before. Keep dealing the cards in sets of six like this until the stock runs out, stopping to move any eligible cards to the foundations at the end of each deal. When your stock of cards runs out, turn all the cards in the reserve face-up, making them all available for building on the foundations.

Once there are no more cards in the tableau or reserve piles to place on the foundations, you are entitled to three re-deals. To begin each re-deal, place the first tableau pile over the second, then over the third and finally the fourth.

Turn the cards face-down and place the reserve piles that remain underneath. Begin the game again, dealing in sets of six as before, until you have exhausted your stock of cards and there are no more eligible cards in the tableau or the reserve piles to move to the foundations. On the third and final re-deal, there is no reserve. Simply deal four cards at a time onto your tableau, face-up. Check at the end of each deal to see if any cards can be moved to the foundations. Continue until the stock of cards runs out.

Finishing the Game

If at the end of your three re-deals you have moved all 104 cards to the foundations, you have won.

DIPLOMAT

This is another double-pack solitaire game in which
eight foundation piles are constructed in ascending
ace-to-king same-suit sequences. In Diplomat, the
tableau takes the form of eight 'fans'.

Equipment: Two packs of playing cards
Rating: Fun to play
Level of Difficulty: Moderate

Setup
Start Diplomat by dealing eight fans, each with four face-
up cards, as in the diagram. As any of the eight aces
appear, set them in a separate foundation row. The cards
remaining after you have your eight fans (a total of 32
cards) form the stock.

Object of the Game
The object of the game is to end up with eight columns of
cards, each column containing a complete suit in ascending
order (A, 2, 3 … J, Q, K) built on the foundation aces.

Playing the Game
The exposed cards on the far right of the fans can either be
used on the foundations or be put together in a descending
sequence (K, Q, J … 3, 2, A) with other exposed cards on
any of the fans, irrespective of color or suit. As the game

continues and you create sequences or part-sequences, you
can move them from one fan to another, but only in
sequence. If you have moved all four cards in a fan, you can
build another using any card that's available in the tableau
and moving only one card at a time.

Once you have made all possible moves in the tableau,
deal from the stock of cards one at a time. If you cannot
play the card to a foundation or the tableau, place it face-up
in a waste pile. The top card of the waste pile is always
available for use. Continue playing until the stock has run
out and there are no more possible moves available.

Finishing the Game
If you have eight complete piles in your foundation cards,
each arranged by suit and ascending order, you have won.

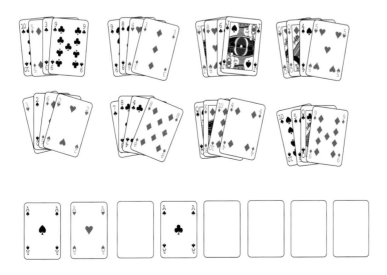

*Tableau and foundations
for Diplomat*

NESTOR

Nestor is won not by augmenting your cards, but by getting rid of them. This is done by removing pairs of cards of the same rank – two deuces or two jacks, for example.

Equipment: A pack of playing cards
Rating: Fair chance to win
Level of Difficulty: Moderate

Setup

Deal 48 cards into eight columns of six overlapping cards each. Watch the cards as you deal: you cannot have two cards of the same rank in the same column. If you already have a card in a pile with the same rank as a card you are about to deal, put the second card at the bottom of the pack, and replace it with the next card of differing rank that you deal from the pack.

After dealing the eight columns for the tableau, you will have four cards remaining. Place them face-up in a row above or below the columns. These four cards act as your reserve.

Object of the Game

The object of the game is to end up with all the cards in one discard pile, by removing all cards from the tableau and reserve in pairs of the same rank.

Playing the Game

The exposed (bottom) cards in each column of the tableau and all the reserve are available for play. Remove pairs of cards of the same rank (e.g. two fives or two kings) wherever you see them in the tableau (or the reserve if there are none in the tableau), and place them in a discard pile. Once these are removed, fresh cards become available in the tableau for you to pair up and discard in their turn.

Finishing the Game

If all the cards in the tableau and reserve have been paired up and discarded, you have won.

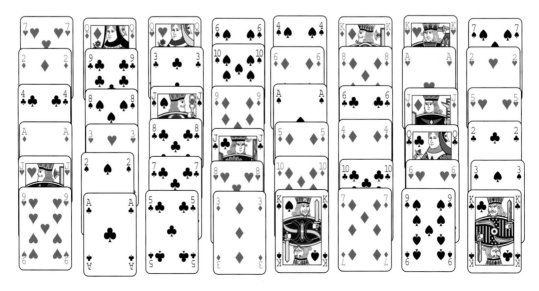

Tableau for Nestor

FORTUNE

Fortune is a single-pack game with a square tableau. Here, the tableau has 12 cards, and the four aces are lined up above it in a row to act as the foundations for ascending suits that run from the aces at the base to the kings at the top.

> **Equipment:** A pack of playing cards
> **Rating:** Needs concentration
> **Level of Difficulty:** Moderate

Setup

To start, find the four aces in the pack and lay them face-up in a row to act as foundations. Below the aces, deal 12 face-up cards in three rows of four cards each, as in the diagram. These cards form the tableau. The remaining 36 cards are the stock.

Object of the Game

The object of the game is to end up with four piles of cards built on your foundation aces, each one arranged in ascending ace-to-king sequence (A, 2, 3 … J, Q, K) by suit.

Playing the Game

Moving one card at a time, use the cards in the tableau to build up sequences on the foundations. You can also play cards within the tableau onto other tableau cards to make up descending same-suit sequences (e.g. 5, 4, 3). Only one card may be moved at a time. Once you have made all possible moves, deal the stock one card at a time. Use suitable cards to build sequences on either the foundations or the tableau. Unsuitable cards are consigned face-up to a waste pile, the top card of which is always available for play. Any gap in the tableau is filled with the top card of the waste pile. If there is no waste pile, use the top card from the stock. Continue until the stock runs out and all possible moves have been made. The stock can be dealt only once.

Finishing the Game

If you have moved all 52 cards to the four foundation piles in the correct ascending sequence by suit, you have won.

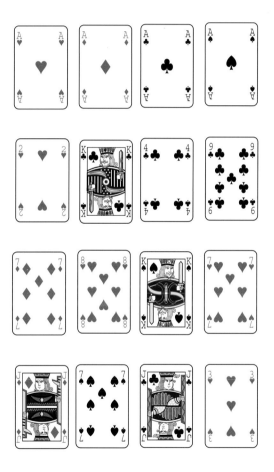

Tableau for Fortune

SWITCHBACK

Switchback doesn't use the kings, which are discarded before play begins. Unusually, Switchback uses a circular tableau, which encloses the four aces that are the foundation for two switching sequences built in opposite directions.

> **Equipment:** Two packs of playing cards, without kings
> **Rating:** Not as hard as it may seem
> **Level of Difficulty:** Challenging

Setup

To start Switchback, discard all the kings (eight in total) from two packs of cards. Take one ace of each suit from the cards and arrange them face-up in a square as in the diagram. These are your foundation cards. Shuffle the remaining cards, then deal a tableau of 12 cards around the aces. The remaining 80 cards are your stock.

Object of the Game

The object of the game is to end up with four foundation sequences, each built by suit as follows: A, 2, 3, 4, 5, 6, Q, J, 10, 9, 8, 7, then in reverse as 7, 8, 9, 10, J, Q, 6, 5, 4, 3, 2, A – hence the name Switchback.

Playing the Game

Use the cards in the circle to build the required sequences on the foundations. Any gaps in the circle can be filled with a card from the stock, or from one of the waste piles when you have them later.

Deal the cards from the stock one at a time, placing any card that cannot be built on one of the foundations or used to fill a gap in the circle on one of the waste piles. You can make up to four waste piles from cards that don't fit into the sequences and use these to fill spaces as they appear. Cards in the waste piles are placed face-up and the top card is always available.

You are allowed to deal the stock only once, but you can take advantage of a grace (a privilege permitting you to make a move that would otherwise be considered illegal) by shuffling each of your waste piles once and playing on, hoping to complete the required sequences.

Finishing the Game

If you have moved all the cards to your foundation aces and built the required sequences on each one, you have won.

Tip

This game is not as difficult as it first appears. You always have the 12 cards in the circle, the top card of each waste pile and the top card of the stock available to move to the foundation as suitable. You will learn to deal cards to your waste pile to the best advantage.

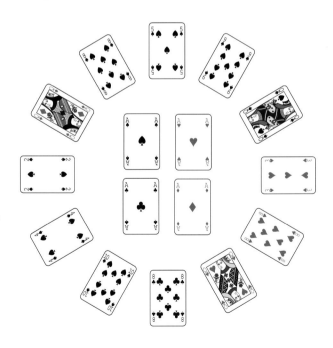

Tableau for Switchback. The deuce of clubs can be played on the ace of clubs, and the space filled with a card from the stock.

ROYAL COTILLION

The cotillion was a popular dance at the French royal court in the eighteenth century. In this double-pack card game, the kings and queens of each suit take part in the dance.

> **Equipment:** Two packs of playing cards
> **Rating:** Keep your wits about you
> **Level of Difficulty:** Challenging

Setup

Start Royal Cotillion by removing one set of aces and deuces from two packs of playing cards. Set these eight cards in two columns as foundations. Next deal 12 cards to the left of the foundations and 16 cards to the right as shown in the diagram. These cards form the 'left wing' and 'right wing' of the game. The remaining cards form the stock.

Object of the Game

The object of the game is to end up with eight piles of cards built by sequence on the foundations as follows: On the aces, build 3, 5, 7, 9, J, K, 2, 4, 6, 8, 10, Q by suit. On the deuces, build 4, 6, 8, 10, Q, A, 3, 5, 7, 9, J, K by suit.

Playing the Game

Only the bottom cards of the columns in the left wing may be built on a foundation and the spaces are not filled. The space makes the next card in the column above the gap available to be moved to a foundation. Any card on the right wing can be built on the foundation, and the resulting space must be filled with the top card from either the waste pile or the stock.

First scan the cards on the left and right wings and move any available cards to the foundations. Fill any gaps on the right wing from the stock. Deal the stock once only, one card at a time, and consign any card that cannot placed on a foundation or used to fill gaps in the right wing face-up to the waste pile. You can use the top card of the waste pile, if eligible, to build on the foundation sequences at any time.

Finishing the Game

If you have moved all the cards to the foundations in the correct sequence, you have won.

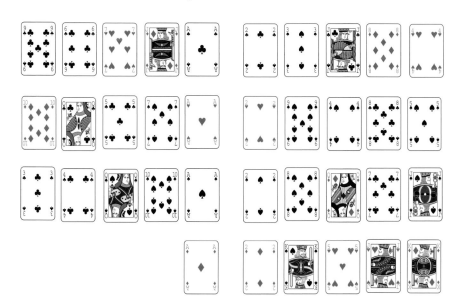

An example tableau for Royal Cotillion. Here the three of clubs can be immediately built on the deuce of clubs, but the space should not be filled with another card from the stock. On the right wing, both the three and four of spades can be built on the deuce of spades. In this case, fill the gaps with new cards from the stock.

PUSS IN THE CORNER

Puss in the Corner is similar to Sir Tommy (page 14) and Strategy (page 52), but it has a different tableau layout. Its tableau has four waste piles, and the aces that form the foundations are arranged in a square.

> **Equipment:** A pack of playing cards
> **Rating:** Needs concentration
> **Level of Difficulty:** Challenging

Setup

Start by taking the four aces from a single pack of playing cards. Place them face-up in a square as in the diagram. These are your foundation cards. Deal another four cards, face-up, placing them at the corner of each ace. These cards form the bases for the waste piles.

Object of the Game

The object of the game is to end up with four ascending sequences (A, 2, 3 … J, Q, K) by color on the foundations.

Playing the Game

Deal four cards, one at a time, from your stock, placing them face-up on any of the waste piles. You don't have to confine yourself to one card on each of the heaps (see tip), and the top cards of the waste piles are always available for building on the foundations. At the end of each deal, check to see if any cards can be moved to the foundations. Cards can be moved only one at a time. Continue dealing from your stock four at a time, moving any suitable cards to the foundation sequences, until the stock runs out. You are entitled to one re-deal only. Put the waste piles together in any order, without shuffling, then deal four at a time as before until you have run out of cards.

Finishing the Game

If you have four complete piles in your foundations, each arranged by color and ascending sequence, you have won.

Tip

It's a good idea to put the higher-ranked cards on a particular waste pile, so you can keep track of where they are. Also, when dealing cards onto the waste piles, wherever possible, play a card on a higher-ranked rather than a lower-ranked card.

Tableau for Puss in the Corner

LOVELY LUCY

The aim of Lovely Lucy, originally a French game, is to construct four sequences of same-suit cards in ascending ace-to-king sequences. It is similar to Shamrocks (see page 45).

Equipment: A pack of playing cards
Rating: Difficult to win
Level of Difficulty: Challenging

Setup

Deal three cards at a time, face-up, into 17 fans as in the diagram. The last card to be dealt (the fifty-second) is placed in the tableau on its own, as shown.

Object of the Game

The object of the game is to end up with four ascending sequences by suit (A, 2, 3 … J, Q, K) in your foundations.

Playing the Game

Only the single (fifty-second) card and the exposed (top) right-hand card of each fan are available for play. As they arise, remove the aces to form the foundations. Next, add any eligible cards to the foundations in an ascending same-suit sequence or move them to any fan to provide descending sequences in the same suit as the fan's exposed

card. Fans can contain more than three cards. Spaces made by moving all the cards in a fan are not filled, and there is no waste pile. When your sequence-building options run out, shuffle the cards remaining on the tableau, and re-deal them in fans of three. (Any leftover cards make a fan of their own.)

You are now entitled to two re-deals. If, after this, you run out of cards to move, you are entitled to take any one card from the tableau with others on top of it and, if possible, place it on an eligible fan or a foundation. This move, which may be made only once, is called 'Merci!' in French, and may enable you to win the game.

Finishing the Game

If you have moved all the cards to the four foundations in ascending ace-to-king sequence, you have won.

Tableau for Lovely Lucy

BAKER'S DOZEN

As we all know, 'baker's dozen' means 13 instead of 12. This comes from the old English practise of putting 13 loaves in an order of a dozen, in order to avoid a fine for short-changing customers. This game was probably named after the 13 columns in its tableau.

Equipment: A pack of playing cards
Rating: Needs concentration
Level of Difficulty: Challenging

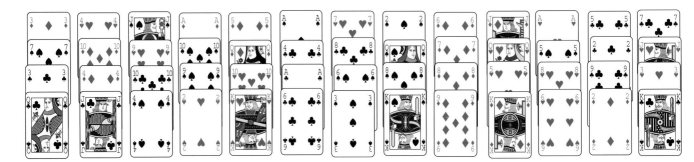

Tableau for Baker's Dozen

Setup

Start Baker's Dozen by dealing out the complete 52-card pack, face-up, in 13 columns of four cards each as shown in the diagram.

Once you have dealt the tableau, move the kings to the bottom of the piles (top of the columns) in which they appear. If you have two or more kings in one column, move both of them, keeping to the same order in which you dealt them.

Object of the Game

The object of the game is to build ascending sequences (A, 2, 3 ... J, Q, K) by suit on each of the four aces, which are placed as a foundation row above the tableau as they become available.

Playing the Game

Only the exposed card at the bottom of each column is available for play and only one card can be moved at a time. Check to see whether any aces are available to move to the foundation row. Once you have moved any available cards,

take the exposed card of a column – any suit, any color – and put it on an eligible exposed card of a different pile. Cards moved within the tableau are arranged by descending sequence only (e.g. 6, 5, 4 ...), regardless of suit. Cards moved to the foundation piles are in ascending order (A, 2, 3 ... etc.) by suit. There is no waste pile. Move any eligible cards to the foundation piles as they appear. Any gaps in the columns are not filled once all the cards in that particular column have been moved to another pile. Continue moving the cards as they are exposed, building up your foundations as you go, until there are no more moves available.

Finishing the Game

If you have moved all your cards to the foundation piles in ascending order by suit, you have won.

Tip

Keep an eye out for two cards of the same suit in a single column. If the higher card is available for play first, it needs to be moved to another column as quickly as possible to make the lower-ranked card available for the foundation.

FORTRESS

Fortress is similar to Beleaguered Castle (see page 11), but is rather more complicated. For one thing, the tableau in Fortress uses more piles of cards.

▌ **Equipment:** A pack of playing cards
▌ **Rating:** Chances of winning are low
▌ **Level of Difficulty:** Challenging

Setup

Start Fortress by dealing a tableau of 10 piles of overlapping cards, arranged in two columns of five, and leaving space between for the aces which will form the foundations. The top two piles should have six cards each, and all the others five cards. Deal the cards from the outside in, so that the exposed (top) card of each pile is closest to the foundations, as in the diagram.

Object of the Game

The object of the game is to end up with four piles of cards in ascending sequence (A, 2, 3 … J, Q, K) by suit in the foundations.

Playing the Game

Cards can be moved only one at a time and, as the aces emerge during the game, they should be placed in the central column (see diagram) to act as foundations. The exposed card in each tableau pile can be placed on the foundations or moved elsewhere in the tableau, wherever it is possible to add to the suit sequences. You can build in ascending or descending order in the tableau, but there is no round-the-corner building. Where spaces appear in the tableau, fill them with any card available to you.

A game of Fortress in its early stages. The deuce of spades can be moved onto the ace of spades, freeing up the deuce of diamonds, which can also be moved to the foundations.

Finishing the Game

If you have moved all the cards to the foundations in ascending sequence, you have won.

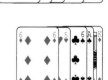

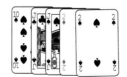

KING'S AUDIENCE

King's Audience, a single-pack game, is also known as Queen's Audience. One possible reason for this is that the four kings and four queens seem to observe the action of the game.

> Equipment: A pack of playing cards
> Rating: Keep a wary eye on the columns
> Level of Difficulty: Challenging

Setup

To start King's Audience, deal 16 cards face-up in a square reserve, known as the antechamber. The space inside it is known as the audience chamber. The remaining cards form the stock. After the cards are dealt, the king and queen of each suit, whenever both become available together, are placed inside the audience chamber, and do not participate in the rest of the game. The jack and the ace of each suit, whenever they become available together, are placed inside the audience chamber with the jack on top; these two become the foundation for each suit. The ace and jack of each suit can *only* be moved to the audience chamber when they are available for play at the same time. The same is true for the king and queen of each suit.

Object of the game

The object of the game is to end up with four descending sequences (J, 10, 9 … 4, 3, 2) by suit in the audience chamber. The aces remain hidden beneath the jacks in the foundation piles, and the kings and queens are arranged in pairs by suit above the foundations.

Playing the Game

The cards in the antechamber are available for play only to the foundations, but they are available at any time. Once an eligible card is taken out of the antechamber and placed on the foundations, replace it with the top card from the waste pile. If there is no waste pile yet, use the top card from your unused stock. When you have made all available moves from the antechamber to the foundations, deal the cards in the stock, one at a time. Play any eligible cards to the foundations as you go, keeping an eye on the antechamber cards to make sure you do not miss a move.

If a card cannot be used, place it face-up on the waste pile. Keep filling the gaps in the antechamber as you go, continuing the game until all the stock has been dealt and no more moves can be made.

Finishing the Game

If all the cards end up in the audience chamber with the kings and queens looking down on the four foundation sequences in descending order by suit, you have won.

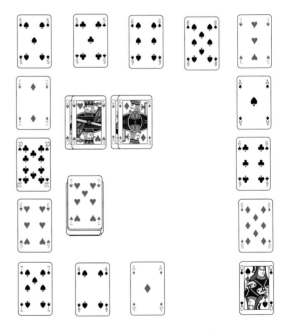

A game of King's Audience. The jack about to be played will become the foundation for diamonds along with the ace.

FROG

Frog, also known as Toad, uses two packs of cards and involves building ace-to-king foundations, regardless of suit. It is also one of the few games of solitaire which boils almost entirely down to your skill in placing the cards.

> **Equipment:** Two packs of playing cards
> **Rating:** Watch those waste piles
> **Level of Difficulty:** Challenging

Setup

Deal 13 cards face-up and arrange them in a single pile. This is your reserve, also known as the Frog. If there are no aces among these 13 cards, take one out from the pack and place it next to the reserve pile as the first foundation. As you come across the other aces during subsequent dealing, these, too, should be placed in a column below the first so that you eventually have eight foundations. The remaining cards form the stock from which you make your waste piles.

Object of the Game

The object of the game is to end up with eight piles of foundation cards arranged in ascending sequence (A, 2, 3 … J, Q, K). Both suit and color are disregarded.

Playing the Game

Form five waste piles by dealing one card at a time, face-up, in a row alongside your first foundation ace as shown in the diagram. Any card you deal can be placed on any waste pile: the choice is yours. Move any eligible top card of any waste pile or the top card in the reserve to the foundations at any time, as long as it fits into the sequence. Continue dealing the stock one at a time until it runs out. Keep an eye on the waste piles and your reserve, moving eligible cards as you go.

Finishing the Game

If you have moved all cards to the eight foundation piles in ascending order regardless of suit or color, you have won.

Tip

There is no re-deal in Frog, so you have only once chance to transfer all the cards onto the foundation piles. To give yourself the best chance of winning the game, it's a good idea to keep a special waste pile for the kings and queens, as these will only block lower-ranked cards as you build your foundation sequences. It is a good idea to try to build your waste piles downwards as much as possible in any case, again so that the higher-ranked cards don't block you from moving lower-ranked ones to the foundations.

Tableau for Frog

AGNES

The aim of Agnes is to build ascending round-the-corner suit sequences on to the foundation cards.

> **Equipment:** A pack of playing cards
> **Rating:** Chances of winning are low
> **Level of Difficulty:** Challenging

Setup

Deal the tableau as in the diagram, then place an extra card, face-up, above the tableau to form the first of four foundation piles. As they become available, the other three cards of the same rank as this one should be placed alongside to form the other foundations. Deal a reserve of seven cards face-up in a row below the tableau. The remaining 16 cards form the stock.

Object of the Game

The object of the game is to end up with four foundation piles in same-suit ascending order (e.g. if the first card of your foundation sequence is a 10, all the foundations will run 10, J, Q, K, A, 2 3 … 7, 8, 9 in their respective suits).

Playing the Game

Play cards from both the tableau and the reserve, building up the foundation columns in ascending suit sequences. Cards can also be placed on the exposed cards in the tableau, in descending sequences of the same color. A sequence can be moved from one column to another, but only if all cards in the sequence are of the same suit. If a tableau column becomes empty, it can be filled with any available card, or a same-suit sequence of cards.

When all possible moves have been made in the tableau and the reserve, use the stock to deal another row of seven cards face-up to the reserve at the bottom of the tableau columns. Gaps in the reserve are not filled until each new deal. After one further deal to the reserve, you'll have two cards left. Deal as if they are a reserve of their own. Play to the foundation or the tableau as eligible. Continue until all possible moves have been made.

Finishing the Game

If you have four complete piles in your foundation cards, each arranged in ascending order by suit, you have won.

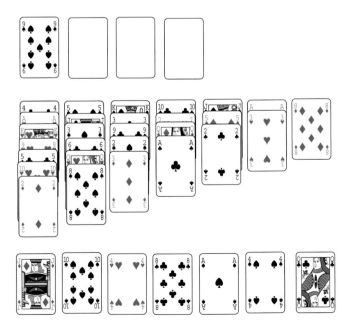

Foundations, tableau and reserve for Agnes

TOURNAMENT

In this double-pack game, named after the armed contests of medieval times, your aim is to build same-suit ace-to-king and king-to-ace sequences.

Equipment: Two packs of playing cards
Rating: Needs concentration
Level of Difficulty: Challenging

Setup

Start Tournament by dealing two columns of four cards each, with plenty of space between the columns. Each column must contain an ace or king, or both. If they don't, shuffle the cards and try again. These columns form the reserve (known as the 'kibitzers'). Once you have the ace and king you need, deal six columns of four overlapping cards in a row between the two columns of four, as shown in the diagram. These cards form the tableau (known as the 'dormitzers'). The remaining cards form the stock. The foundations will be built in a row of eight across the bottom as cards become available.

Object of the Game

The object of the game is to free one ace and one king of each suit, and build on them by suit. Aces are built up and kings are built down, so that you end up with eight foundation piles, four in ascending order (A, 2, 3 … J, Q, K) and four in descending order (K, Q, J … 3, 2, A)..

Playing the Game

The exposed (bottom) cards on each column in the tableau and all the cards in the reserve are available. The cards in the reserve can be built on the foundations, and any spaces left are filled with any available card from the tableau. The piles in the reserve can hold only one card at a time, and spaces do not need to be filled immediately, but may be done so at your discretion. Cards in the tableau cannot be built on each other, only on the foundations or in a space in the reserve. If a tableau column becomes empty, fill the space with a new set of four cards dealt from the stock. Also, the top cards of the foundations can be built on each other, which is useful when two foundations of the same suit meet.

After making all possible moves, deal four cards at a time from the stock onto each column in the tableau. Keep dealing from the stock in this manner, making all available moves as you go, until the stock runs out. When play comes to a standstill, collect all the cards in the six tableau columns into a single pile, gathering the piles from right to left and placing them one on top of the other. Without shuffling, deal six new columns of four cards each to the tableau. Continue the game as before until there are no more moves. This can be done twice in the game.

Finishing the Game

If you have moved all the cards to the eight foundation piles in the correct order, you have won.

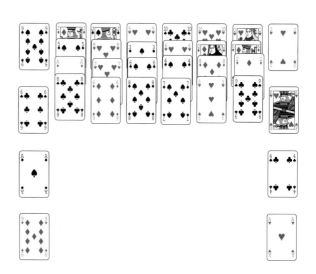

Tableau for Tournament

INTRIGUE

Intrigue is similar to Salic Law (see page 42), except that, in this case, the queens take part in the game. Intrigue, which uses two packs of cards, is concerned with building sequences on foundations, but has an unusual way of doing it.

Equipment: Two packs of playing cards
Rating: Unusual foundation building
Level of Difficulty: Challenging

Setup

Place a queen as the base for the first tableau pile. Set all the fives and sixes in two rows above the queen as foundations. The remaining cards form the stock.

Object of the Game

The object of the game is to end up with 16 sequences built on these fives and sixes. The top row of fives is built on in descending sequence from five to king (5, 4, 3 2, A, K) and the second row of sixes is built in ascending sequence from six to jack (6, 7, 8, 9, 10, J). All foundations are built without regard to suit or color.

Playing the Game

Deal the stock one at a time onto the queen at the far right of the tableau until you find another queen. This forms the base card for the second tableau pile in the row. Continue in the same manner until you have all eight queens in the tableau, with cards dealt onto them in piles. The exposed (top) card of each tableau pile is available for building the sequences at any time. Cards that are eligible for the foundations (initally fours and sevens) are available as you deal and can be immediately placed on the foundations.

Keep going until your stock runs out and all eligible cards are on the foundations. But remember, you can't build on cards in the tableau. A pile that has a queen on her own is 'empty' and you can place any card on it.

Finishing the Game

If you have moved the cards to the 16 foundations in the correct sequences, with the face cards on top in each case, you have won.

A game of Intrigue in progress. A three dealt from the stock now can be built on the four of spades.

GAPS

Gaps is a widely known solitaire game in which the whole pack is dealt into a 52-card tableau at the beginning. The game is also known as Spaces, Vacancies, Clown Solitaire, Blue Moon, and Montana.

Equipment: A pack of playing cards
Rating: This is a game of chance, so winning's not easy
Level of Difficulty: Challenging

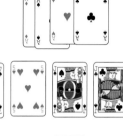

Tableau for Gaps

Setup

Deal all 52 cards into a tableau of four rows of 13 cards each, as in the diagram.

Object of the Game

The object of the game is to end up with four rows of twelve cards, in ascending order (deuce through king) by suit.

Playing the Game

Remove the aces and fill the gaps left over with cards from elsewhere in the tableau. These must be of the same suit, and ranked one higher than the card on the left of the space. For example, in the first row of the diagram above, the jack of hearts would move into the gap. Leave an empty gap on the right of a king, and fill any gap on the far left of the tableau with a deuce (two). Now fill the gaps you have just created with other cards, and continue until you have made all possible moves.

Gather up all cards which are not yet in their final correct sequence, and shuffle these with the aces. Then redeal these cards into the gaps in the tableau. Remove the aces and continue as before. You can re-shuffle and re-deal only twice.

Finishing the Game

To win the game, you must have all 48 cards laid down in number order with only one suit per row. This is very much a game of chance, however, so winning isn't all that easy.

PERSEVERANCE

No one knows why this game is called Perseverance. Perhaps the name indicates the characteristic you need in abundance to play it to a conclusion – win or lose!

> **Equipment:** A pack of playing cards
> **Rating:** Perseverance required
> **Level of Difficulty:** Challenging

Setup

Start by removing the four aces from the pack and placing them in a row to form foundations. Shuffle the remaining 48 cards and deal them into 12 piles of four face-up cards each (you can deal the cards either one at a time or in groups of four). These cards form the tableau.

Object of the Game

The object of the game is to end up with four foundation piles arranged in ascending order (A, 2, 3 …J, Q, K) by suit.

Playing the Game

The exposed (top) card of each tableau pile is available for play. These cards can be placed on the foundations, which are built up by suit (A, 2, 3 …J, Q. K), or on another of the tableau piles, which are built down (e.g. 5, 4, 3, 2) by suit. You can move only one card at a time, unless you have built

a sequence on a tableau pile, in which case you can move it as a unit to another tableau pile if eligible. Gaps that develop in the tableau are not filled.

After you have built on the piles as far as you are able, you are entitled to two re-deals. Take the twelfth pile of the tableau and put it on top of the eleventh pile and so on in reverse order until a large single pile is formed. Don't shuffle the cards, but deal them again, this time four cards at a time, into piles of four face-up cards each. Any leftover cards are dealt as a separate pile.

Continue play as before, until all possible moves have been made after the second re-deal.

Finishing the Game

If you have moved all the cards in the tableau to the foundation piles in ascending order by suit, you have won.

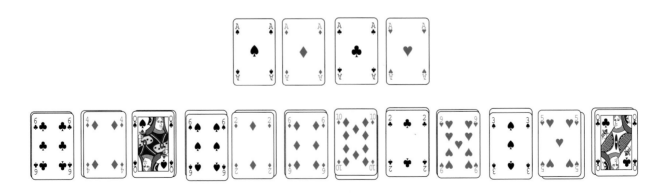

Tableau for Perseverance

ALHAMBRA

Alhambra is a double-pack game in which you build ascending ace-to-king suit sequences and descending king-to-ace suit sequences. You are allowed to deal three times in all, and packets of cards serve as the tableau.

Equipment: Two packs of playing cards
Rating: Keep your wits about you
Level of Difficulty: Challenging

Setup

Start Alhambra by removing one ace and one king of each suit (eight in total) from two packs of cards. Lay them out in a row as foundations for the suit sequences. Next deal eight piles of four cards each, face-up, and put them in a row below the foundation cards. These cards form the reserve, or packets. The remaining 64 cards are the stock.

Object of the Game

The object of the game is to end up with eight piles arranged by suit in your foundations. Four of these are in ascending order from ace (A, 2, 3 …J, Q, K); the other four are in descending order from king (K, Q, J …3, 2, A).

Playing the Game

Deal your stock of unused cards one at a time. Place those that can contribute to a suit sequence on the relevant foundation and consign the rest face-up to a waste pile. The top card of the waste pile is available at any time to build on a foundation, as are the top cards of the eight piles in the reserve. Reserve cards can also be placed on the top card of the waste pile if they contribute to an ascending, descending, or round-the-corner suit sequence. Don't build sequences on the reserve and don't fill any spaces appearing in the reserve when all four cards in a pile have been placed elsewhere. Continue playing until the stock runs out, moving any eligible cards to the foundations as you go.

You are now entitled to two re-deals using the waste pile. Pick up the waste pile, turn over and use as the new stock. Keep playing as before, one card at a time, until there are no more possible moves.

Finishing the Game

If you have moved all the cards to the eight foundation piles, four in ascending order (A to K) and four in descending order (K to A) by suit, you have won.

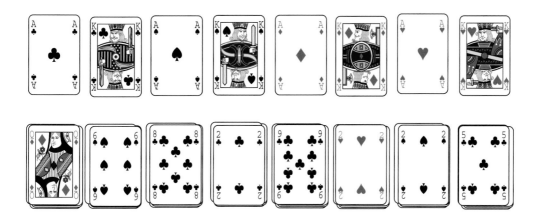

Tableau for Alhambra

NAPOLEON'S SQUARE

This double-pack game of solitaire has a tableau that is shaped like three sides of a square, with the bottom side open. The object of Napoleon's Square is to build ascending same-suit ace-to-king sequences in the center of the square.

Equipment: Two packs of playing cards
Rating: Use your judgment
Level of Difficulty: Challenging

Setup

Start by dealing 48 cards, face-up, in 12 piles of four cards each, along the three sides of a square as in the diagram. These cards form the tableau. As any ace emerges during dealing, place it in the center of the square as a foundation and replace with the next card from the pile. The remaining cards form the stock.

Object of the Game

The object of the game is to move all the aces to the center of the unfinished square as they become available and build eight ascending sequences (A, 2, 3 …J, Q, K), each arranged by suit, on the foundation aces.

Playing the Game

The top cards of each pile in the square are exposed and can be placed on the foundations in ascending sequence. They can also be moved to the other piles in the square to form descending suit sequences. Cards in sequence at the top of a pile can be moved as a unit and placed on other piles or on the foundations. (You are allowed to look at all the cards in a pile when making your moves.) Any spaces which appear in the square can be filled by dealing a card from the stock, by taking a card or a sequence of cards from another pile, or by using the top card of the waste pile.

Deal the stock one card at a time. Any card that is ineligible for building on the foundations or cannot be moved to a pile in the tableau is consigned face-up to a waste pile. The top card of the waste pile is always available, and the stock is dealt only once. Continue dealing the stock until you run out of cards and there are no more possible moves.

Finishing the Game

If you have moved all the cards to the foundation aces in the correct ascending sequence by suit, you have won.

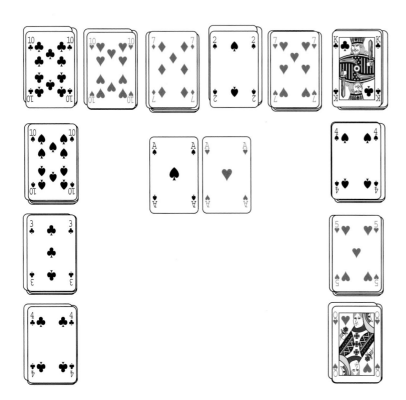

Tableau for Napoleon's Square

ROYAL RENDEZVOUS

In this double-pack game of solitaire, deuces (twos) feature alongside aces as the foundations. You can use all 16 cards in the tableau to build three differently arranged sequences.

Equipment: Two packs of playing cards
Rating: Needs concentration
Level of Difficulty: Challenging

Setup

To start Royal Rendezvous, remove all eight aces and one deuce (two) from each suit to form the foundations. Arrange the aces and the deuces in the format shown in the diagram. Next, deal four rows of four cards each below the foundations to form the tableau. The remaining cards form the stock.

Object of the Game

The object of the game is to end up with twelve ascending same-suit foundation sequences running like this: a) four complete ace-to-king suit sequences (A, 2, 3 ... J, Q, K) in the upper row; b) four ascending suit sequences running A, 3, 5, 7, 9, J, K in the second row; and c) four ascending suit sequences on the deuce foundations running 2, 4, 6, 8, 10, Q.

Playing the Game

You can use any of the tableau cards to build on a foundation if eligible. Any vacancies in the tableau are filled from the waste pile; if there is no waste pile, fill the spaces in the tableau from your stock.

Once you have made all possible moves in the tableau, deal the stock one card at a time. Move cards to the foundation as eligible, placing any cards that can't be used face-up on a waste pile. The top card of the waste pile is always available to be moved to a foundation, if eligible. Continue until the stock has run out and all possible moves have been made. There are no re-deals.

Finishing the Game

If you have moved all the cards to the foundation in the correct ascending same-suit sequences, you have won.

Tip

It is not necessary to move cards from the tableau to the foundations just because they are eligible. Every time you do so, you have to fill the space from the waste pile or the stock. Try to fill the tableau with lower-ranked cards, so that they don't become blocked from use by being buried in the waste pile. Higher-ranked cards can be played to the waste pile more readily, as you can use them later in the game.

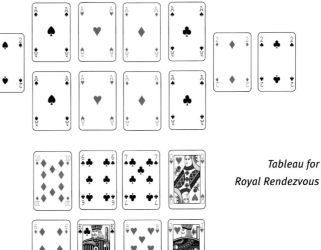

Tableau for Royal Rendezvous

ROYAL PARADE

In the double-pack game Royal Parade, aces don't take part. Any that emerge on to the tableau while you're dealing should be put aside. In their place deuces (twos) will receive a bit of the limelight, by occupying the top row in the tableau.

Equipment: Two packs of playing cards
Rating: Not your straightforward game of solitaire
Level of Difficulty: Challenging

Setup

Start by dealing 24 cards, placing them in three rows of eight cards each, as shown in the diagram. The remaining cards form the stock.

Object of the Game

The object of the game is to rearrange the tableau so that you have eight deuces (twos) in the top row, eight threes in the middle row and eight fours in the bottom row. From there, you build suit sequences from cards numbered or valued as follows: on the deuces, place 5, 8, J; on the threes place 6, 9, Q; on the fours, place 7, 10, K.

Playing the Game

Discard any aces from the tableau. Move any suitable cards to fill the spaces left by the aces. For example, if you have a gap in the top row and a deuce (two) in one of the other rows, move the deuce to fill the gap and form a foundation, and so

on. Look at the tableau again and move any eligible cards of the correct suit to fit the desired sequence. For example, if you have a three of clubs in the second row and a six of clubs anywhere in the tableau, move the six of clubs onto the three.

When you have completed all possible moves, deal another eight cards face-up into a separate reserve below the tableau. Use the cards to build on the foundations or fill spaces in the tableau. Deal the next eight cards from the stock to each of the eight reserve piles, and continue as before. You can move cards from the reserve piles to the foundations at any time, but only if they are the top cards in the pile. Continue dealing and playing until your cards run out and all possible moves have been made.

Finishing the Game

If you have discarded all the aces and moved the remaining 96 cards to the tableau in the right sequences, you have won.

Tableau for Royal Parade

MISS MILLIGAN

Miss Milligan is a classic two-pack game. The idea is to build ascending ace-to-king suit sequences. However, if you get stuck, Miss Milligan offers a secret weapon that could help you win the game.

Equipment: Two packs of playing cards
Rating: Has a secret ploy to overcome problems
Level of Difficulty: Challenging

Setup
Start by dealing eight cards, face-up and side by side, as in the diagram. These cards form the tableau. Move any aces to a row of foundation cards above the tableau. The remaining cards form the stock.

Object of the Game
The object of the game is to end up with eight piles built on your foundation aces, arranged by suit and in ascending order (A, 2, 3 … J, Q, K).

Playing the Game
Move any eligible cards from the tableau to the foundation aces or a sequence. You can place cards within the tableau on each other in descending sequence by alternating color. Only kings can be moved into gaps created in the tableau.

When you cannot build up the foundation sequences and have no suitable cards to place in the tableau, deal eight more cards onto the tableau piles or in the spaces, and proceed in the same way as before. You can move any card or sequence from one pile to another, as long as you stick to the black-red color pattern. Aces are removed to the foundations as you go, and they are available to be built upon at any time. Keep dealing the stock, eight at a time, until it runs out.

Once you have used up your card stock and made all possible moves, a maneuver known as 'waiving' may come to the rescue. Pick a single top card from the tableau and keep it in your hand as you continue trying to build on the foundations or the tableau. If you are lucky, the card you have waived could provide the vital link that enables you to complete a sequence. If not, put the waived card back on the pile it came from, waive another card and keep trying. Only one card may be waived at a time.

Finishing the Game
If you have moved all the cards to the foundation aces in the correct ascending sequences, you have won.

Tip
Keep an eye on the sequences in your tableau piles as you are playing. Sometimes transferring part of a sequence can help you to reveal useful cards previously blocked from play, particularly when you have reached the waiving section of the game. For example, you may have a run of cards starting with a red queen and a red queen exposed in another tableau pile. Moving the black jack downwards (rather than the whole sequence) may allow you to reveal a better run of cards for moving to the foundation or within the tableau.

Tableau for Miss Milligan

FLOWER GARDEN

Flower Garden consists of six fans of six cards each (the beds), while the remaining 16 cards form a reserve (the bouquet). The aim is to separate out the aces and, in a row above the beds, build on them in ascending sequences by suit, from aces to kings.

> **Equipment:** A pack of playing cards
> **Rating:** Requires concentration
> **Level of Difficulty:** Challenging

Setup

Start by dealing six fans of six cards each for the beds and 16 cards for the bouquet, as shown in the diagram. You can hold the cards in the bouquet in your hand if you wish.

Object of the Game

The object of the game is to move all eight aces to a foundation row above the beds and build on them in ascending sequence (A, 2, 3 … J, Q, K) by suit.

Playing the Game

Only the exposed (top) card in each fan is available, but all the cards in the bouquet are on hand to play at all times. Bouquet cards can be built on the foundations or played on top of the exposed cards in the beds in descending sequence without regard to suit or color. You can also move a part-sequence from one bed to another, but remember to keep the cards in sequence while doing so. Vacant spaces that appear once a bed has been cleared of cards can be filled in either by using a card from the bouquet or moving an exposed card or sequence of cards from another bed. Continue playing until you have made all possible moves.

Finishing the Game

If you have moved all 52 cards to the foundation piles in the correct ascending sequence by suit, you have won.

Tip

If at all possible, avoid playing cards from the bouquet onto a bed as this reduces the number of cards you have to choose from when making a play. The same applies to leaving an empty bed. Also, try not to build too many cards on one bed as you may trap lower-ranked cards below higher-ranked ones. Your first and primary aim should be to release the lower-ranked cards (A, 2, 3) as quickly as possible. If these are blocked, winning will be very difficult.

Six Beds for Flower Garden

Bouquet for Flower Garden

KLONDIKE

Klondike is a variant of Agnes (see page 66) and uses the same tableau. The aim is to build up four ascending ace-to-king sequences of the same suit.

Equipment: A pack of playing cards
Rating: Keeps you on your toes
Level of Difficulty: Challenging

Setup
Start Klondike by dealing a tableau of 28 cards in seven columns as shown in the diagram. The card at the bottom of each column is dealt face-up. The remaining 24 cards form the stock.

Object of the Game
The object of the game is to end up with four piles in the foundation, arranged by suit in ascending order (A, 2, 3 … J, Q, K).

Playing the Game
Remove any aces to act as foundations and place them in a row above the columns. Turn up the card that was underneath the ace. Exposed cards at the bottom of a column can be used to build on a foundation, or placed in a descending sequence of alternating colors in the tableau. You may move a sequence from one tableau column to another only as a whole and when it can be placed in sequence.

Once a face-up card has been played, turn the face-down card immediately above it to face-up. When an entire column is empty, only a king may fill the space, with or without its sequence attached. Aces must be immediately played to the foundation row, but you can keep other eligible cards in position on the tableau if you think you may have a better move further into the game.

Once you have made all possible moves in the tableau, deal the stock one card at a time, face-up, to a waste pile. The top card of the waste pile can be used for foundation building or placed in sequence on a column in the tableau. Continue playing until the stock runs out, keeping an eye on possible moves in the tableau so that you can ensure that you free all the face-down cards from their columns. You are entitled to only one deal in Klondike.

Finishing the Game
If you have moved all 52 cards to the four foundation piles in the correct ascending sequence by suit, you have won.

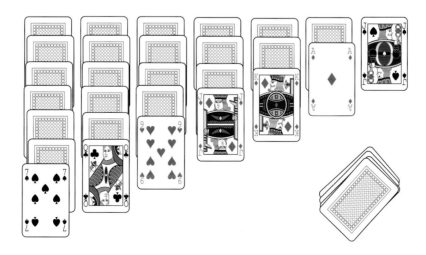

Tableau for Klondike

BIG BEN

Big Ben is a rather more complex version of Grandfather's Clock (see pages 22–23) on a larger scale.

> **Equipment:** Two packs of playing cards
> **Rating:** Needs concentration
> **Level of Difficulty:** Challenging

Setup

Before you start, remove from the pack the twelve cards shown in the inner circle on the diagram opposite and lay them out in the same way. Start with the two of clubs at the nine o'clock position and proceed round the clock face to the king of diamonds at eight o'clock. These cards form the foundations.

Once this inner circle is complete, deal a tableau of 12 piles of three cards face-up in an outer circle. At this stage, you have distributed 48 cards to the inner and outer circles, so you will have 56 remaining to act as your stock.

Object of the Game

The object of the game is to end up with the top card of each pile of the inner circle matching its hour on the clock face. This is done by building up piles of cards in sequence and by suit. For example, a six of hearts should top the pile at the six o'clock position, with the pile containing the sequence J, Q, K, A, 2, 3, 4, 5, 6 of hearts.

Playing the Game

Move any exposed (top) eligible cards from the outer circle, or tableau, to the inner circle, or foundations, where they are are built in ascending sequence (e.g. 2, 3, 4) by suit. Cards can also be built in descending sequence (e.g. 4, 3 2) by suit on the outer circle piles, and moved to the inner circle when required.

Gaps in the outer circle, or piles with fewer than three cards in them, can be filled with cards from the stock. You can choose when to fill these gaps. Once you can make no further moves and there is at least one outer pile with fewer than three cards on it, deal twelve cards from your stock clockwise, starting at the 12 o'clock pile, placing one card on each pile. Once all the piles in the outer circle have a minimum of three cards, you can carry on building up the sequences.

Inevitably, there will be cards that you can't build onto the piles in either the inner or the outer circle. These should be placed in a waste pile and there they remain because they can't be used to fill gaps. You are not allowed to re-deal the cards in Big Ben, so, once you have used up all your cards, the game ends.

Finishing the Game

If the top card of each pile is numbered to match its hour on the clock face and is in the correct suit, you have won.

Tableau for Big Ben

NINETY-ONE

This game is really a number puzzle. Ninety-one requires some deft mental arithmetic to conclude with a score of 91 – the aggregate of the numbers on the cards in the tableau.

| **Equipment:** A pack of playing cards
| **Rating:** Bring your calculator
| **Level of Difficulty:** Challenging

Setup

To start Ninety-One, deal a pack of playing cards face-up into 13 piles, four cards to each pile.

Object of the Game

The object of the game is the end up with a total of 91 when you add together the numerical value of all the cards across the tableau. Jacks count as 11, queens count as 12 and kings count as 13.

How to Play

To reach the total of 91 and win the game, you need to add up the numerical values of the cards on top of the tableau piles. If the cards don't reach this total, try moving one card from the top of a pile to the top of another pile. You can move cards between the piles as often as you wish, but you must retain the total of 13 piles at all times. Keep going until the cards on top of the piles add up to 91 – or until you've had enough arithmetic!

Tableau for Ninety-One

WINDMILL

The double-pack game of Windmill, which is also called Propeller, gets its names from its simple cross-shaped tableau. In Windmill, you don't have to bother about matching suits or colors because the value of the cards is what counts.

> **Equipment:** Two packs of playing cards
> **Rating:** Needs concentration
> **Level of Difficulty:** Challenging

Setup

In this version of Windmill, a king is placed at the center of the tableau as the primary foundation, and aces are placed in the four angles of the cross, as the secondary foundations. In another version, the roles and positions of the kings and aces are reversed.

Start the game by laying out the cross-shaped tableau, but, at this early stage, without the aces shown in the diagram; they come into play later. Place any king face-up, and deal two cards above it, two below and two on either side. The king is the base for the first foundation; the other eight cards form the reserve.

Object of the Game

The two purposes of Windmill are a) to build a descending round-the-corner sequence, using all 52 cards of one pack (i.e. build four sequences of K, Q, J … 3, 2, A, disregarding suit and color), and b) to build ascending ace-to-king (A, 2, 3 … J, Q, K) sequences on the four aces, also regardless of suit and color.

Playing the Game

Move any eligible cards from the reserve to the central king foundation or, if available, to an ace foundation. Gaps in the reserve can be filled from the waste pile, if you have one. If not, fill any gaps from your unused stock of cards. Once you have made all possible moves from your reserve, deal the cards from the stock one at a time to a waste pile. Place eligible cards on the king foundation in the center of the cross. Building the four ace foundations begins once four aces have revealed themselves in play and have been moved to the foundations, as indicated in the diagram. Another way of building sequences at this stage is to move a card from one of the secondary ace foundations to the primary king

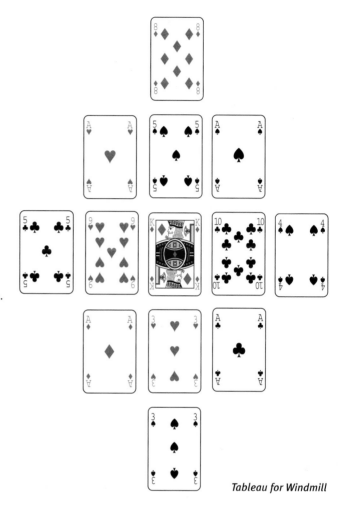

Tableau for Windmill

foundation. But this comes with a condition: the next card you place on the king foundation has to come from the waste pile or the reserve.

When you have run out of opportunities to build the sequences, and you have gone through your stock of cards, Windmill doesn't offer you a second deal, but there is a second chance. Pick up the waste pile and deal the first card. If you can place it on a foundation, do so, then deal another card and keep going for as long as you can place the waste-pile cards on a foundation. If you turn up a waste-pile card that can't be placed on a foundation, the game is over.

Finishing the Game

If you have moved all the cards to the foundations (52 on the king foundation and 13 on each of the ace foundations), you have won.

HEADS AND TAILS

In this game, the top line of eight cards is 'heads' and a third line of another eight cards is 'tails'. In between is a row of eight packets of 11 cards each. The object of the game is to create four ascending ace-to-king suit sequences and four descending king-to-ace suit sequences.

| **Equipment:** Two packs of playing cards
| **Rating:** Proceed with care
| **Level of Difficulty:** Challenging

Setup

Start Heads and Tails by dealing three rows of cards. The top and bottom rows should each have eight face-up cards as shown in the diagram. The middle row should have 8 piles of 11 face-up cards. These cards form the tableau of heads (top), packets (middle) and tails (bottom).

Object of the Game

The object of the game is to build eight piles arranged by suit on the foundations. Two sets of each of the four suits are represented. One set consists of four piles in ascending ace-to-king sequence (A, 2, 3 … J, Q, K), while the other set consists of four piles in descending king-to-ace sequence (K, Q, J … 3, 2, A).

Playing the Game

As they appear in dealing, move the foundation aces and kings to a separate foundation row, building on them as

eligible cards become available. Once you have dealt, only the cards in the rows of heads and tails can be used to build on the foundations, but you can also stack cards in the heads and tails in ascending, descending or round-the-corner sequences, switching sequences as needed. The cards from the middle row are used to fill the spaces in the heads and tails rows. When taking cards from the middle to fill gaps in the other two rows, you are allowed to take only those cards that are immediately above or below the space. If, as the game progresses, you find that all the cards in a packet have been used up, you can take a card from any of the other packets and use it in your quest to complete the sequences. Continue until all possible moves have been made.

Finishing the Game

If you have moved all the cards to the foundations in the correct ascending and descending sequences by suit, you have won.

Tableau for Heads and Tails

STALACTITES

In this game, you aren't allowed to build sequences of cards in one column onto another, only onto the foundations. But you can do that regardless of the suits to which the cards belong.

Equipment: A pack of playing cards
Rating: You can decide the building method
Level of Difficulty: Challenging

Setup

Start Stalactites by dealing four cards face-up to form the foundations, as in the diagram. These cards don't have to be of the same rank. (Sometimes players turn the four cards sideways on the tableau, stacking the other cards upright onto them, so that they can always see the value of the card with which the foundation starts.) Deal the other 48 cards face-up into eight columns, six overlapping cards to each one. These cards form the tableau.

Object of the Game

The object of the game is to build ascending sequences on the four foundation cards regardless of suit or color. You can do this in one of two ways, either in ones (A, 2, 3, 4 and so on up to K) or in twos (A, 3, 5, 7, 9, J, K, 2, 4, 6, 8, 10, Q). Choose one form of sequence and stick with it for all the foundations; do not vary between the two. Foundations are built round the corner, from ace to king (if building by ones) or from ace to queen (if building by twos). For example, if you are building by ones and your foundation card is a jack, the sequence will be J, Q, K, A, 2 ... 8, 9, 10. Or, if you are building by twos and your foundation is a six, the sequence will be 6, 8, 10, Q, A, 3, 5, 7, 9, J, K, 2, 4.

Playing the Game

The exposed card at the bottom of each column in the tableau is available for play. Move eligible cards from the tableau to the foundations to build the sequences. Any gaps that develop in the tableau are not filled. When you run out of moves from the tableau to the foundations, you are entitled to place two exposed cards in the

tableau in a reserve. Cards in the reserve must be built on a foundation when possible. They can't return to the tableau and there's room for only two cards in the reserve at one time. This maneuver can prove extremely useful in freeing trapped cards in the tableau columns. Continue until all possible moves have been made.

Finishing the Game

If you have moved all the cards to the foundations in the correct ascending sequence, you have won.

Tip

Keep an eye on exactly which cards you will be freeing when you move cards to the reserve. Choose the best option for freeing cards that will enable you to continue; otherwise play will quickly come to a standstill.

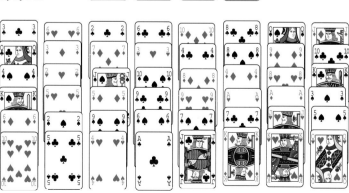

Tableau for Stalactites

BIG BERTHA

In Big Bertha, 90 cards are dealt as the tableau, with the other 14 in reserve. Big Bertha is another name for the queen. The aim of the game is to build ascending same-suit sequences to the queens from the aces, which are placed at the base of the foundation piles.

Equipment: Two packs of playing cards
Rating: Use your judgment
Level of Difficulty: Challenging

Tableau for Big Bertha

Setup

Deal a tableau of 90 cards in 15 columns of six face-up overlapping cards each as in the diagram. You can hold the other 14 cards in your hand or lay them out on the table as your reserve.

Object of the Game

The object of the game is to free the eight aces and use them to form foundations. These are then built on by suit in ascending sequence to the queen (A, 2, 3 … 10, J, Q). Kings are discarded as they appear and take no further part in the game.

Playing the Game

The exposed cards at the bottom of the columns and the cards in the reserve can be built on the foundations, where appropriate. You can also build descending sequences in alternating colors on the bottom cards of the columns in the table, and you may move an existing sequence from the foot of one column to another, as long as you keep to the correct order and alternating color. If all the cards in a column have been moved, fill the gap with a single card or a sequence that you have already constructed. Move eligible cards so that you can release the aces and move them to the foundations for building. Continue building the foundations until there are no more possible moves.

Finishing the Game

If you have moved all the cards from the tableau and reserve to the foundations in the correct ascending same-suit sequences, you have won.

Tip

Choose carefully when you are faced with two options of the same-value card. One may be more useful than the other in freeing cards for the foundations.

LE CADRAN

Cadran is French for 'face' – not a human face, but the sort that appears on a clock or sundial. The aim of Le Cadran is to use the eight aces as foundation cards and, from there, build ascending sequences, by suit, to the kings.

> **Equipment:** Two packs of playing cards
> **Rating:** A build-up game that needs care
> **Level of Difficulty:** Challenging

Setup

Start by setting all eight aces in a foundation row. Next, deal a tableau of 10 columns of four face-up cards underneath the foundation, as shown in the diagram. The remaining cards form the stock.

Object of the Game

The object of the game is to end up with eight piles built on the foundation aces, each arranged in ascending ace-to-king sequences (A, 2, 3 …J, Q, K) by suit.

Playing the Game

The exposed card of each column is available to be moved to the foundations as eligible. Cards must be moved one at a time, not in sequences. Place them directly onto the foundations, as long as they fit the sequence, or move them to one of the tableau columns to add to a descending suit sequence. Once you have made all possible moves, deal the stock one card at a time. Play any eligible cards to the foundation or add to a tableau column in sequence, placing any ineligible cards face-up in a waste pile. The top card of the waste pile is always available for play. If a tableau column becomes empty, fill it with either an exposed card from another column or with the top card of the waste pile. Continue dealing until the stock runs out and there are no more possible moves. The stock can be dealt only once.

Finishing the Game

If you have moved all the cards to the foundations in the correct ascending same-suit sequences, you have won.

Tableau for Le Cadran

BISLEY

Bisley is a single-pack game of solitaire that uses all 52 cards for the tableau. The aim of the game is to build same-suit sequences ascending from ace to king and descending from king to ace.

> **Equipment:** A pack of playing cards
> **Rating:** Proceed with care; the big tableau can be confusing
> **Level of Difficulty:** Challenging

Setup

Start Bisley by placing the four aces face-up in a row. Deal nine cards in the same row, starting to the left of the last ace. After that, deal a further three rows of 13 cards each below the first row as in the diagram.

Object of the Game

The object of the game is to end up with all the cards arranged by suit on the foundation aces and kings. Cards on the aces should be in ascending sequence (A, 2, 3 … etc.). Cards on the kings should be in descending sequence (K, Q, J … etc.). It does not matter where the sequences meet.

Playing the Game

As the kings appear in the deal, set each one above the ace of its own suit. Only the bottom cards in the columns are available for play. They can be used to build on either an ace or king foundation, placed in sequence on the bottom card of another column, or have another card placed on them. Sequences can be built either up or down by suit. Spaces left in the columns after the last card is removed are not filled. Continue packing and moving cards to the foundations until there are no more possible moves.

Finishing the Game

If you have moved all the cards to the eight foundations in correct ascending and descending order, you have won.

A game of Bisley in its early stages. The queen of diamonds can be built on the king of diamonds. The jack of clubs is also available for play.

CONGRESS

In this game, you play the eight aces to the center, and use them as foundations for building ascending sequences to the kings.

| **Equipment:** Two packs of playing cards
| **Rating:** Needs plenty of patience
| **Level of Difficulty:** Challenging

Setup

Start Congress by dealing eight cards face-up in two columns of four cards. If any aces appear, play them to the center to build on as foundations and replace in the tableau with the next card dealt from the stock. The cards left over after dealing form the stock.

Object of the Game

The object of the game is to end up with eight piles built on the foundation aces, each arranged in ascending ace-to-king sequence (A, 2, 3 … J, Q, K) by suit.

Finishing the Game

Deal the cards from your stock one at a time, constructing a tableau in descending sequences by their face value, regardless of suit. Cards in the tableau can be built on the foundations or onto another card in the tableau, but only one card may be moved at a time. Any card that can't be put on the tableau or built on the foundations is played face-up a waste pile. The top card of the waste pile is always available for play.

Gaps in the tableau must be filled with the next card from your stock or with the top card of the waste pile. Here, you have a choice. You are allowed to look at the next card of the stock to decide whether you want to use it to fill a gap in the tableau or would prefer to use the top card from the waste pile. Continue playing until the stock runs out and there are no more possible moves. There is no re-deal.

Winning the Game

If you have moved all the cards to the foundations in the correct ascending sequence by suit, you have won.

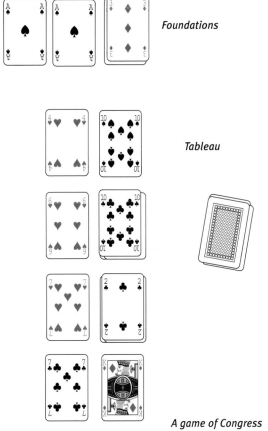

Foundations

Tableau

A game of Congress

FOUR SEASONS

The aim of Four Seasons is to build round-the-corner ascending suit sequences.

> **Equipment:** A pack of playing cards
> **Rating:** Needs concentration
> **Level of Difficulty:** Challenging

Setup

Start Four Seasons by dealing a cruciform (cross) of five cards as in the diagram. Next, deal a sixth card to the upper left-hand corner of the cross. This will be the base for the first of four foundations. The three other cards of the same rank are placed as foundations at the other three corners of the cross as they become available in the game. The remaining cards form the stock.

Object of the Game

The object of the game is to end up with four foundation piles, each one arranged by suit in ascending round-the-corner sequence according to the first foundation card in place. For example, if the value of your first foundation card is nine, the sequence will be 10, J, K, A, 2, 3 ... 7, 8, 9. If you start with an ace, it will simply run in the usual ascending sequence (A, 2, 3 ... J, Q, K).

Playing the Game

Build eligible cards in the cross tableau in descending order – don't worry about the suit. As with the foundations, tableau cards are built round-the-corner. The top card in each pile in the tableau is available for play. Sequences cannot be moved in a unit – only one at a time. Fill spaces that appear in the tableau with any available cards (the top card of a pile in the cross, the top card of the waste pile or the top card from the stock). When you have made all possible initial moves, deal the cards from the stock one at a time, keeping an eye out for the remaining foundation cards. Cards that don't fit into a foundation sequence or on the tableau should be put face-up in a waste pile. The top card of the waste pile is always available for play. Continue until the stock runs out and all possible moved have been made. There is no re-deal.

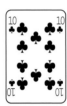

Tableau and first foundation for Four Seasons

Finishing the Game

If you have moved all the cards to the foundations in the correct round-the-corner sequences by suit, you have won.

DIEPPE

Dieppe is another double-pack game of solitaire and, like Congress (see page 87), features foundation piles with ascending ace-to-king sequences. There are eight tableau piles, with three cards in each of them, and eight foundation piles.

Equipment: Two packs of playing cards
Rating: Keep concentrating
Level of Difficulty: Challenging

Setup
Start Dieppe by removing the eight aces and laying in a row to form the foundations. Deal eight columns of three face-up overlapping cards each, as shown in the diagram. These cards form the tableau.

Object of the Game
The object of the game is to end up with eight piles built on the foundation aces, each arranged in ascending ace-to-king sequence (A, 2, 3 …J, Q, K) by suit.

Playing the Game
The cards at the bottom of each column are available for play to either the foundation or elsewhere within the tableau. Sequences within the tableau are built, either ascending or descending, irrespective of suit or color. Sequences within the tableau can be moved as a whole or in part from one column to another, as long as they fall in the correct sequence. Gaps in the tableau columns are filled by any exposed card or sequence of cards.

When there are no more moves within the tableau, deal the stock one card at a time. Cards that do not fit onto the tableau sequences or the foundations are consigned face-up to a waste pile. The top card of the waste pile is always available. Continue until the stock runs out and all possible moves have been made. There are no redeals.

Finishing the Game
If you have moved all the cards to the foundations in the correct ascending sequence by suit, you have won.

In this illustration, the two and three of clubs have already been taken from the tableau and placed on the foundation. Now more cards from the tableau can be placed on the foundations. To do this, they need to be freed up by moving cards around on the tableau. For example, by placing the five of hearts on the six of spades, the two of spades is freed to be moved to the foundations.

SULTAN

Sultan, a double-pack game of solitaire, is also known as Emperor of Germany. Sultan seems more apt, however, as the tableau is called the 'divan'. In this game, the idea is to build up suit sequences from seven of the eight kings to the queens.

> **Equipment:** Two packs of playing cards
> **Rating:** You need skill for this one
> **Level of Difficulty:** Challenging

Setup

Start Sultan by removing the eight kings and one of the aces of hearts from the pack. Deal eight cards to form the 'divan', in two columns of four with space enough for three cards between them. The kings and the ace of hearts form the central 'block' of nine cards as shown in the diagram. With the exception of the king of hearts (which is the 'sultan') in the middle of the block, they are used as foundations for suit sequences. The cards in the divan are used to build the sequences.

Object of the Game

The object of the game is to build eight piles on the foundation kings and ace of hearts, ignoring the king of hearts in the centre. Each foundation is arranged by suit and built in ascending sequence to the queen (K, A, 2 …10, J, Q for the kings; A, 2, 3 … 10, J, Q for the ace).

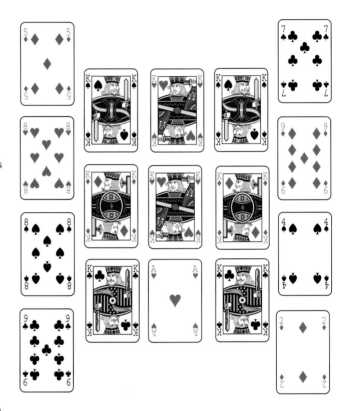

Tableau for Sultan

Playing the Game

Move all eligible cards from the divan to the foundation. Spaces in the divan can be filled with cards from the stock or the waste pile, but you do not need to do this right away (see tip). Deal the stock one card at a time, moving any eligible cards to the foundation. Cards that cannot be used are consigned face-up to a waste pile. The top card of the waste pile is always available for play.

Once the stock of cards has run out and all possible moves have been made, pick up the waste pile, shuffle and re-deal face-up to a waste pile as before. This can be done a second time if necessary.

Finishing the Game

If you have moved all the cards to the foundations in the correct ascending sequence by suit, and the queens are surrounding the king of hearts, you have won. Inevitably, some cards will end up on the waste pile because they don't fit the sequences, but these have a second (or third) chance to participate later on in the game because you can re-deal the cards from your waste pile twice.

Tip

Careful use of the divan is central to this game. Think before you fill spaces that appear here, bearing in mind which cards you are likely to need while you are dealing in relation what is in your foundations at any given time. Perhaps you have a built a foundation up to a five, but both sixes have already been discarded to the waste pile. Putting any higher-ranked cards of the same suit would be a waste because they would serve no purpose.

CROSSWORD

Crossword emulates its namesake by using the picture cards to block off a sequence, just as black squares in the puzzle block off words. But arithmetic also comes into it.

> **Equipment:** A pack of playing cards
> **Rating:** Bring along your calculator
> **Level of Difficulty:** Challenging

Setup

Start Crossword by removing the jacks, queens and kings from the pack. Set them to one side for the moment. The remaining cards form the stock and are played one card at a time.

Object of the Game

The object of the game is to finish with a square of seven cards by seven cards. Each horizontal and vertical row of cards within the square must add up to an even number. Only the numbered cards are counted towards this total – picture cards are disregarded.

Playing the Game

Deal the first card of the stock face-up onto the table. Continue dealing one card a time, building up a tableau with the cards as you go. Cards must be placed in adjoining positions to the cards already in the table, at the bottom or top, to one side or diagonally. Keep an eye on your math as you go. The picture cards function in much the same way as a black square in a crossword (hence the game's name) and are placed as needed so that each row will add up to an even number at the end. You will use at least nine if not all of them. Eventually, you

This diagram shows the game Crossword about halfway through, with 26 cards in place. There are four complete horizontal rows (nos. 3, 4, 5, 6) and two complete vertical columns (nos 3 and 4) in which the non-picture cards add to even numbers. The three of hearts (top left) is about to be added, at the same time, to the first horizontal row and the second vertical row, but more cards will be needed if the row and the column are each going to add up to an even number.

will have one space left to fill and four cards left over in your stock. Look at the remaining unplaced cards and, hopefully, choose the one that is needed to complete the game.

Finishing the Game

If you have a seven by seven square of 49 cards where all the rows add up to an even number (discounting picture cards), you have won.

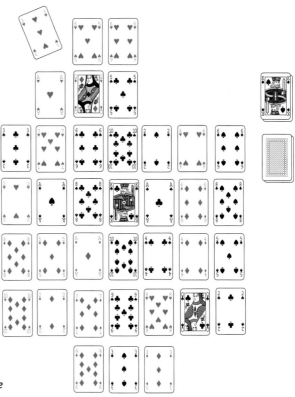

CAPTIVE QUEENS

Captive Queens is a variant of another game of solitaire called Quadrille. Its purpose is to have the four queens in a cross flanking the kings and jacks of each suit above, below and on either side.

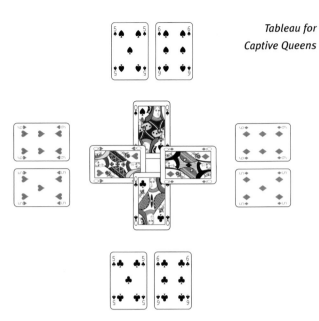

Tableau for Captive Queens

| Equipment: A pack of playing cards
| Rating: Keep your wits about you
| Level of Difficulty: Tough

Setup

Start Captive Queens by removing the four queens and forming them into an overlapping cross as in the diagram. Next, remove the fives and sixes of all four suits and set them in matching suits above, below and on each side of the queens as shown. The remaining cards form the stock.

Object of the Game

The object of the game is to end up with eight piles in the foundations arranged by suit and topped with a jack or a king. Four piles are in ascending sequence six to jack (6, 7, 8, 9, 10, J). The other four are in descending sequence five to king (5, 4, 3, 2, A K).

Playing the Game

Deal the stock face-up one cards at a time into a waste pile, moving eligible cards to the foundations as you go. The top card of the waste pile is always available. When the stock has run out, turn the waste pile over without shuffling. You are allowed two re-deals.

Finishing the Game

If you have moved the cards to the foundations in the correct ascending and descending sequences with a jack or king at the top, respectively, you have won.

CRAZY QUILT

Crazy Quilt is also known as Quilt, Indian Carpet or Japanese Rug. The aim of the game is to move all the cards onto the foundations, which comprise one ace and one king of each suit.

| Equipment: Two packs of playing cards
| Rating: Watch the tableau carefully
| Level of Difficulty: Tough

Setup

Remove an ace and a king of each suit from the double pack of cards: these form the foundations. Deal the remaining cards in eight rows of eight cards each as in the diagram.

Once glance at it will tell you why some players think the finished tableau, also known as the reserve, looks like a crazy quilt. The remaining 32 cards form the stock.

Object of the Game

The object of the game is to end up with eight piles in the foundations. Four are arranged by suit in ascending sequence from the aces (A, 2, 3 … J, Q, K) and four are arranged by suit in descending sequence from the kings (K, Q, J … 3, 2, A).

Playing the Game

Cards in the quilt which have one short side free can be placed on the foundations. For example, in the first row of the diagram, the queen of clubs can be placed on the king of clubs, but the queen of spades cannot be moved onto the king of spades. Once the queen of clubs is moved, the two cards either side are available to be moved to the foundations. Spaces made in the tableau are not filled, and there is no building of cards in the tableau.

Deal the cards from the stock one at a time. Cards that cannot be moved to the foundations are placed face-up on a waste pile. The top card of the waste pile is always available to be moved to the foundations. Also, available cards in the tableau can be built onto the top card of the waste pile in ascending or descending round-the-corner sequences by suit.

Once the stock runs out, pick up the waste pile and turn it face-down without shuffling. This now becomes your new stock and enables you to play on, but you are only entitled to do this once in a game. Continue as before until all possible moves have been made.

Finishing the Game

If you have moved all the cards to the foundations in the correct ascending and descending sequences by suit, you have won.

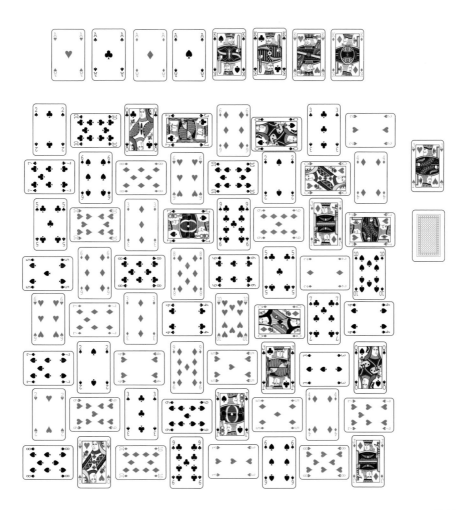

Tableau for Crazy Quilt

LE CHATEAU

Le Chateau ('the castle' in French) is a double-pack game of solitaire with an unusual layout in which cards are dealt in 12 packets of five cards each. The purpose of Le Chateau is to build ace-to-king sequences by suit.

| **Equipment:** Two packs of playing cards
| **Rating:** Need skill and concentration
| **Level of Difficulty:** Tough

Setup

Start Le Chateau by dealing the cards in successive rows of three, four and five packets of cards, with spaces between them, as shown in the diagram. Each packet should contain five cards each. The remaining cards form the stock.

Object of the Game

The object of the game is to end up with eight piles built on foundation aces by suit, each one arranged in ascending ace-to-king sequence (A, 2, 3 … J, Q, K).

Playing the Game

Move the aces to the center to act as foundations as they appear while dealing. The exposed (top) cards of each packet are used to build on foundations. Or you can place them on each other in alternating colors and in descending sequence. Sequences can be moved from one packet to another as a whole or in part if you wish, but you must retain the color pattern.

Deal the cards from the stock one at a time. Play directly to a foundation or onto a packet in the tableau if you can. If you can't, place face-up on a waste pile. The top card of the waste pile is always available for play. If you use up all the cards in a packet, fill the space with the top card of the waste pile or a single card, complete sequence, or partial sequence, from one of the other packets in the tableau. Continue dealing and playing until the stock run out and there are no more possible moves. There are no redeals.

Finishing the Game

If you have moved all the cards to the foundations in the correct ascending sequence by suit, you have won.

Tableau and foundations for Le Chateau

KING ALBERT

It is believed that this single-pack game of solitaire was named after King Albert I of Belgium (1875–1934). The purpose of the game is to build four ascending sequences by suit from the aces to the kings. The game is also known as Idiot's Delight.

Equipment: A pack of playing cards
Rating: Skill and intelligence required
Level of Difficulty: Tough

Setup

Start King Albert by dealing 45 cards face-up into a nine-column tableau as in the diagram. The first column has nine cards, the second has eight, and so on, until the ninth has only one card. The seven remaining cards form the reserve and can be held in your hand or placed face-up on the table.

Setup

The object of the game is to end up with four piles built on the foundation aces, each one arranged in ace-to-king sequence (A, 2, 3 … J, Q, K) by suit.

Playing the Game

The cards at the bottom of each column are exposed and can be used to build on the foundations or moved to other columns in the tableau in descending sequences of alternating colors. Only one card at a time can be moved. The cards in the reserve are also available to be built on foundations or on the exposed cards in the tableau. If a column in the tableau becomes empty, you can fill it with any available card.

In the diagram you will see aces in the columns. These need to be released in order to start the foundations. This will happen when they reach the bottom of their respective columns after all the cards below them have been removed and used. Continue playing until there are no more possible moves.

Finishing the Game

Only one in 10 games ends with all the cards piled on the foundations, perhaps earning the game its alternate name. If, however, you have moved all the cards to the foundations in the correct ascending sequence by suit, you have won.

Tableau for King Albert

THIRTEENS

Also known as Five Piles and Baroness, Thirteens uses a single pack and requires a certain amount of mental arithmetic.

> **Equipment:** A pack of playing cards with the kings removed
> **Rating:** How's your mental arithmetic?
> **Level of Difficulty:** Tough

Setup

Start by removing the four kings from the pack. These take no part in the game. Next, deal five cards face-up in a row as in the diagram. These act as the bases for the five piles of cards that will be built up during the game. The remaining cards form the stock.

Object of the Game

The object of the game is to end up with 24 pairs of discarded cards (and hence no leftover cards), with each pair totalling 13 when their value is added up. Jacks are valued at 11 and queens at 12.

Playing the Game

Look at the cards in the tableau. Remove any two cards that together add up to 13 and set aside in a discard pile. As gaps appear in the tableau, fill them with the top cards of other piles. If you do not have enough cards to do this, fill the spaces from your stock of unused cards. Eventually, you will find that you've filled all the spaces and have no kings or pairs of cards adding up to 13. At this point, deal out another five cards from your stock, placing one on each of the five piles. Keep playing in the same way as before until you have used up your stock of cards and there are no more possible moves.

Finishing the Game

If you have discarded all 48 cards in pairs totalling 13 by face value, you have won.

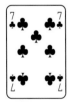

Tableau for Thirteens

PYRAMID

The initial tableau of this game is a pyramid of rows that overlap, with one card at the top and seven cards at the base. Pyramid has the unusual aim of discarding all the cards in the pack by the end of the game, but chances of winning are only about one in fifty.

Equipment: A pack of playing cards
Rating: Not easy to win
Level of Difficulty: Tough

Setup

Start Pyramid by dealing 28 cards face-up in seven rows, beginning with one card at the top and adding a card per row so that you build a pyramid with seven cards at the bottom. It is important that the cards overlap as in the diagram. The remaining 24 cards form the stock.

Object of the Game

The object of the game is to discard the entire pack in pairs of a face value totalling 13, with the exception of the kings. These are discarded singly, as their face value is considered to be 13. Jacks are valued at 11 and queens are valued at 12.

Playing the Game

Only exposed cards can be discarded. Initially, this means the cards in the bottom row of seven. This is where Pyramid becomes tricky. Unless you are discarding a king somewhere in the exposed row of the tableau, you can only discard in pairs adding up to 13. And you only have access to the cards in row above once you have removed a pair of cards so that the card lying above is exposed.

Once any possible moves have been made, deal the stock face-up one at a time onto a waste pile. The top card of the waste pile is exposed and can be paired with a pyramid card or the next card you deal from your stock. Continue until the stock runs out and there are no more moves available. There are no redeals.

Finishing the Game

If you have moved all the cards to the discard pile in the requisite pairs (with the kings moved singly), you have won.

Tableau for Pyramid

MARTHA

In this single-pack game, the tableau uses alternating rows of face-up and face-down cards arranged in 12 overlapping columns. The purpose of Martha is to build ascending suit sequences from the Aces up to the Kings.

Equipment: A pack of playing cards
Rating: Keep your wits about you
Level of Difficulty: Tough

Setup

Start by removing the aces from the pack and setting them in a foundation row. Deal the tableau in 12 columns of four cards each as shown in the diagram. The first and third rows are dealt face-down; the second and fourth rows are dealt face-up.

Object of the Game

The object of the game is to end up with four piles built on the foundation aces, each one arranged in ascending sequence (A, 2, 3 … J, Q, K) by suit.

Playing the Game

The bottom cards of the columns can be used to build on the foundations if eligible. They can also be used to form descending sequences in alternating colors on other exposed cards in the tableau. As long as you retain the number order and alternating colors, you can move a sequence or part-sequence from one column to another. If a space appears in a column, however, only a single card can be used to fill it, not a sequence. Face-down card are turned up when they reach the bottom of a column after the cards below them have been played elsewhere. Continue playing until there are no more possible moves.

Finishing the Game

If you have moved all the cards to the foundations in the correct ascending sequence by suit, you have won.

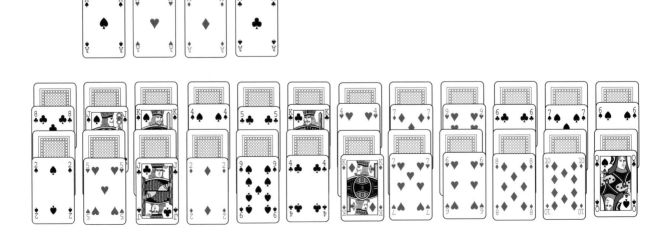

Tableau for Martha

SPIDER

Spider (which is not to be confused with Spiderette) is said to have been the favorite solitaire game of U.S. President Franklin D. Roosevelt when he wanted to take a break from the stress and tension of World War II.

Equipment: A pack of playing cards
Rating: Analyze your moves before making them
Level of Difficulty: Tough

Tableau for Spider

Setup

Start Spider by dealing 40 cards in 10 columns of four overlapping cards each as in the diagram. Only the bottom row of cards is placed face-up. These cards form the tableau. The remaining cards form the stock.

Object of the Game

There are no foundation cards or waste pile in Spider. The object of the game is to build four descending king-to-ace sequences (K, Q, J ... 3, 2, A) by suit within the tableau. Completed sequences are discarded when they are finished, so that ideally you end up with a playing area where there's not a card to be seen.

Playing the Game

All exposed cards in the tableau are available for play and can be built on any other exposed card in descending sequence, regardless of suit or color. When you move a card from one column to another to help build a sequence, turn the newly exposed card face-up. It is now available for play

where appropriate. Once all the cards have been moved from a column, fill the space with any face-up card or with a sequence. While you can build sequences regardless of suit or color, only sequences that are all the same suit can be moved as a unit. When all possible moves have been made and all available spaces are filled, deal 10 cards from your stock, placing one face-up at the bottom of each column. Keep going until your stock has run out and there are no more possible moves.

Finishing the Game

If you have assembled all your cards in the correct descending sequences by suit and discarded them, leaving a tableau clear of cards, you have won.

INTERREGNUM

In the double-pack game of Interregnum, you build eight foundations of 13 cards each in round-the-corner fashion. The method you use to build the foundations, however, is somewhat unusual.

> **Equipment:** Two packs of playing cards
> **Rating:** Unusual foundation building
> **Level of Difficulty:** Tough

Setup

Start by dealing eight cards face-up in a row as in the diagram. These are known as the indicator cards. Each card here will represent the last card in a foundation pile and the space below it will house the foundation pile itself. Leave enough space below the indicator row to add the foundations, then deal another row of eight face-up cards. These cards form the tableau. The remaining cards are your stock.

Object of the Game

The object of the game is to build eight foundations on the (initially vacant) row below the indicator cards. Foundations are built in ascending round-the-corner sequences regardless of suit, and start with the card ranked one higher than the card above it in the indicator row. For example, if the indicator card is a five, the foundation sequence will be 6, 7, 8, 9, 10, J, Q, K, A, 2, 3, 4, 5.

Playing the Game

Cards in the tableau are available only to be moved to the foundations. There is no sequence building or moving cards from one pile to another within the tableau, and the top card only is available for play. Move any eligible cards to the foundation row, then deal eight cards one at a time from the stock, placing one on each tableau pile (or space). Continue dealing eight cards in this manner, putting one card on each of the tableau piles and stopping between each deal to move any

eligible cards to the foundations. Moving a card to the foundations from the tableau pile frees up the card below for play. Keep going until the stock runs out and there are no more possible moves.

When you have put the twelfth card in place on a foundation pile, take the indicator card above it and place it on top of the pile as your thirteenth foundation card. With that, you have 'closed' the pile.

Finishing the Game

If you have closed the pile on all your foundations in the correct round-the-corner sequence, you have won.

This diagram shows the state of play in Interregnum after three deals of cards onto the tableau. The king of spades just dealt to the tableau can be built on either of the queens in the middle foundation row.

CURDS AND WHEY

With Curds and Whey your aim is to build four descending king-to-ace suit sequences, but without using foundations.

> **Equipment:** A pack of playing cards
> **Rating:** A lot of rules to remember
> **Level of Difficulty:** Tough

Setup

Deal the pack into 13 columns of four overlapping face-up cards each as in the diagram. These cards form the tableau.

Object of the Game

There are no foundations in Curds and Whey. The object of the game is to form four descending king-to-ace sequences (K, Q, J ... 3, 2, A) by suit.

Playing the Game

The exposed card at the bottom of each column is available for play. A card can be played in only two ways: a) over a card that is of the same suit and a higher rank (i.e. descending suit

sequence); or b) over a card that is of the same rank but a different suit (e.g. six of hearts played on six of clubs). One card is moved at a time unless a sequence has been made. A sequence of cards (either built down by suit, or in a sequence of cards with the same rank) can be moved in part or as a whole, following the rules above for the bottom card in the sequence. When a column becomes empty, it can be filled only by a king or a sequence starting with a king. Continue until there are no more possible moves.

Finishing the Game

If you have moved all the cards into the correct king-to-ace sequences by suit, you have won.

Tableau for Curds and Whey

MAZE

The tableau for Maze uses everything but the kings. The aim is to arrange the cards in four ascending ace-to-queen suit sequences beginning with the ace at the northwest corner in the top row and ending with a queen in the southeast corner of the bottom row.

Equipment: A pack of playing cards
Rating: Sharpen your skills
Level of Difficulty: Tough

Setup

Start by dealing all 52 cards, including the Kings, face-up into two rows of eight cards each and four of nine cards each as in the diagram. This leaves a space at the end of the first and second rows. Next, remove and discard the kings to create four spaces within the tableau.

Object of the Game

The object of the game is to rearrange the 48 cards remaining in the tableau in four ascending ace-to-queen (A, 2, 3 …10, J, Q) sequences by suit. The sequences begin with an ace at the far left of the top row of the tableau and end with a queen at the far right of the bottom row. Sequences run from left to right along each row, continuing from one row to the next.

Playing the Game

There are several rules to be remembered with Maze. First, only one card may be moved at a time. When filling spaces, make sure that the card you move is in suit sequence and one rank higher than the card to its left, or one rank lower than the card to its right. A space to the right of a queen must be filled with an ace or a same-suit card one rank lower than the card on the right of a space. Also, the bottom is considered to be continuous with the top row (i.e. the last card of the bottom row is 'next to' the first card of the top row.)

Finishing the Game

If you have rearranged all the cards so that you have four consecutive sequences running left to right in ascending order ace to queen, you have won.

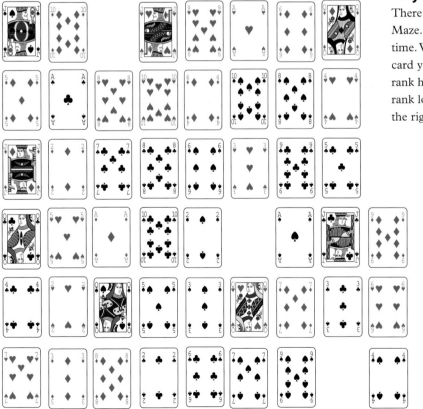

Tableau for Maze

SCORPION

Scorpion is aptly named: it can deliver a sting. The aim is to build descending king-to-ace sequences in suits. Unusually, any card in the tableau can be moved, not just the exposed cards, but the whole column below it must move too.

> **Equipment:** A pack of playing cards
> **Rating:** Think carefully before you make a move
> **Level of Difficulty:** Tough

Setup

Start Scorpion with a 49-card tableau laid out as in the diagram. Put aside the three cards that are left over – these are your reserve.

Object of the Game

The object of the game is to build four descending king-to-ace sequences (K, Q, J … 3, 2, A) within the tableau.

Playing the Game

Build on exposed cards at the bottom of the columns with the next lowest ranked card in the same suit. If you find a same-suit card ranked one lower than a card along the bottom of the columns, place it on that card in descending sequence. If the card is face-up anywhere else in a column, all the cards below it must be moved along with it.

Turn face-down cards face-up when they reach the bottom of a column. Fill empty columns with kings, also moving any cards below them too. When there are no more moves available, deal your three reserve cards face-up, placing one each at the bottom of the first three columns. Keep building until there are no more possible moves.

Finishing the Game

If you have moved all the cards into the correct descending king-to-ace sequences by suit, you have won.

Tip

Think carefully before you make any moves. Consider what lies ahead in the game in terms of several moves rather than just one. One ill-considered play on your part could easily block any chance you have of winning.

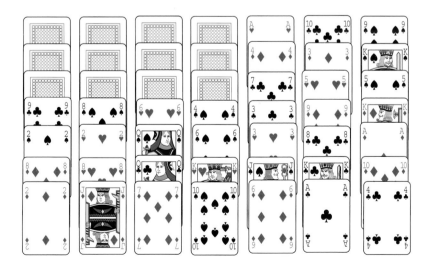

Tableau for Scorpion. In this example, the six of diamonds in the fifth column can be built on the seven of diamonds. The ten of diamonds in the seventh column can be built on the jack of diamonds, but the four of clubs must be moved with it.

QUEEN OF ITALY

The double-pack game of solitaire known as Queen of Italy is also called Terrace. Be warned, though. Queen of Italy isn't all that easy to win.

Equipment: Two packs of playing cards
Rating: Low chance of winning
Level of Difficulty: Tough

Setup

Start by dealing a row of 11 overlapping face-up cards as in the diagram. This is your reserve, or terrace. Below that, leave a space for the foundations, then deal a row of four face-up cards to start the tableau. Choose and remove one tableau card to start the first foundation, then deal another card from your stock to fill the space. Add five more cards to make up a nine-card tableau.

Object of the Game

The object of the game is to build eight foundation piles, each built from the same rank as the first foundation, arranged in alternating color and ascending sequence. (Use the round-the-corner method where necessary, depending on the card chosen for your first foundation.)

Playing the Game

As the other seven cards of the same rank as your first foundation card emerge in dealing, place them in the foundation row. Build sequences on the foundations in alternating colors, using the round-the-corner method where necessary. For example, if your foundation card is a jack, the order will run J, Q, K, A, 2, 3 … 8, 9, 10, in alternating colors. Tableau cards can also be built on other cards in the tableau, still in alternating colors, but this time in descending order. Fill any gaps which appear in the tableau from your stock. You are only allowed to use the top (exposed) card in each pile for building purposes.

The terrace can also be used to build sequences, but only on the foundations themselves. Only the exposed card in the terrace can be played.

When there are no more moves within the tableau, deal your stock face-up one at a time to a waste pile. The top card of the waste pile is always available to play, either to the foundations or to the piles in the tableau. Any card can be used to fill a gap in the tableau. Continue until the stock runs out and there are no more possible moves.

Finishing the Game

If you have moved all your cards to the foundations in the correct ascending (round-the-corner) sequences of alternating colors, you have won.

Tableau for Queen of Italy

MRS MOP

Mrs Mop is a double-pack game where all 104 cards are used to form a rather oversized tableau. The idea is to build eight king-to-ace descending sequences, not on foundations, but within the tableau.

Equipment: Two packs of playing cards
Rating: Not as easy as it looks
Level of Difficulty: Tough

Setup

Start Mrs Mop by dealing 13 columns of eight overlapping face-up cards as shown in the diagram. These cards form the tableau, in which you build the foundations.

Object of the Game

The object of the game is to end up with eight piles of cards built in king-to-ace descending sequences (K, Q, J …3, 2, A) by suit within the tableau.

Playing the Game

The cards at the bottom of the columns can be built on each other in descending sequences. You need not bother about suits or colors: the sequences consist of cards stacked in number order, or in the case of the picture or face cards, in value order. Move only one card at a time unless you have

two or more cards in sequence by suit. In this case, you must move the cards together. After all the cards in a column have been placed elsewhere, fill the space with another card or a suit sequence, if you have one. Continue until there are no more possible moves.

Finishing the Game

If you have moved all the cards into the correct descending king-to-ace sequences by suit, you have won.

Tip

On the face of it Mrs Mop appears to be a fairly easy game, but appearances are deceptive. You will improve your chances of success if you 'mop up' a column of cards early on in the game. The space this leaves makes it easier for you to transfer cards from one column to another.

Tableau for Mrs Mop

CAPRICIEUSE

The aim of Capricieuse is to build eight same-suit sequences, four of which are ascending ace-to-king piles, while the other four are descending king-to-ace piles.

> **Equipment:** Two packs of playing cards
> **Rating:** Use your skill
> **Level of Difficulty:** Tough

Setup

Start by dealing an ace and a king of each suit as the foundations as shown in the diagram. Then deal 12 cards face-up to act as the basis of the tableau. You must deal any eligible card to the foundations as it appears, rather than placing it in the tableau. Keep dealing on the 12 tableau piles in turn, until you have dealt all the cards. To avoid holes in the tableau, cards dealt straight to the foundations are replaced in their relevant tableau pile by the next card to be dealt even if consecutive dealt cards are dealt directly to the foundations.

Object of the Game

The object of the game is to end up with eight same-suit foundation piles. One set of four is built in ascending ace-to-king sequence (A, 2, 3 … J, Q, K). The other is built in descending king-to-ace sequence (K, Q, J … 3, 2, A).

Playing the Game

Building sequences within the tableau starts only after all the cards have been dealt. Use cards from the top of each pile to build on the foundations, or onto another pile within the tableau in ascending or descending same-suit sequence. Sequences cannot be round-the corner, but you can reverse a sequence in the same pile. Move only one card at a time, and use any card to fill the space left by an empty pile.

Continue until you have made all possible moves. You are then entitled to two re-deals. Pick up the piles, starting with the last one you dealt and finishing with the first. Start the game again, dealing and playing as before, until you there are no more possible moves. Re-deal as necessary and once again continue in the same manner.

Finishing the Game

If you have moved all the cards to the foundations in the correct ascending and descending sequences, you have won.

Tableau for Capricieuse

ODD AND EVEN

This double-pack game gets its name from the foundation cards used for its same-suit sequences. The 'odd' number, the ace, is one, and the 'even' number, the deuce (two), is the other.

Equipment: Two packs of playing cards
Rating: Keep careful track of foundation building
Level of Difficulty: Tough

Setup

Start Odd and Even by dealing a reserve of nine cards in three rows of three face-up cards each as shown in the diagram. The remaining cards form the stock.

Object of the Game

The object of the game is to end up with eight same-suit foundations. There should be two sets of four foundations, each containing an ascending sequence of each suit. One set starts with an odd number (ace) and the other with an even number (deuce). Aces run as A, 3, 5, 7, 9, J, K, 2, 4, 6, 8, 10, Q. Deuces run as 2, 4, 6, 8, 10, Q, A, 3, 5, 7, 9, J, K.

Playing the Game

The aim is to remove one ace and one deuce (two) from each suit from either the reserve or the stock as they appear and use as foundations. Once you have checked your reserve for eligible cards, deal the stock face-up one at a time, building on the foundations with any eligible cards turned up there. Cards that don't fit into sequences during dealing are discarded face-up to a waste pile, where the top card is always available to play. Reserve cards are also available to build on the foundations. Any spaces left in the reserve should be filled by the top card of your waste pile or, if you don't have one, the next card from your stock.

When your stock has run out, you are entitled to one re-deal using the waste pile. Simply turn the pile over and deal as before, but without shuffling first. Continue until these cards run out and there are no more possible moves.

Finishing the Game

If you have moved all your cards to the foundations in the correct ascending sequences by suit, you have won.

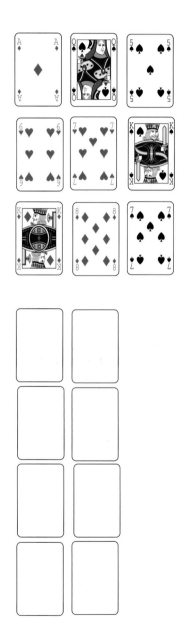

Reserve and foundation spaces for Odd and Even

MATRIMONY

The aim of Matrimony is complex. The idea is to build an ascending suit sequence, round-the-corner style, from the queen to the jack of diamonds, and descending suit sequences from the jacks to the relevant, same-suit queens, and on four tens to the same-suit jacks.

> **Equipment:** Two packs of playing cards
> **Rating:** An unusual game
> **Level of Difficulty:** Tough

Setup

Start Matrimony by dealing 16 cards in two rows of eight as in the diagram. These cards form the tableau. As they appear during dealing, set one queen and one jack of diamonds above the tableau as foundation cards. Do the same with the two jacks of hearts and the four black tens. The rest of the cards represent your stock.

Object of the Game

The object of the game is to end up with eight foundation piles as follows. An ascending round-the-corner sequence (Q, K, A, 2 …8, 9, 10, J) by suit is built on the queen of diamonds. Descending round-the-corner sequences (J, 10, 9, 8 …2, A, K, Q) by suit are built on the jack of diamonds and the two jacks of hearts. Descending round-the-corner sequences are also built on the four black tens (10, 9 8, 7 …A, K, Q, J) by suit.

Playing the Game

Use the cards in the tableau to build on the foundations. Once you have made all possible moves from the tableau to the foundations, deal another 16 cards face-up from the

stock on top of the remaining tableau cards or in spaces left within the tableau. Keep playing as before, moving exposed cards to the foundations as eligible, until your stock of cards runs out.

When there are no more moves available, pick up the pile at the far right of the bottom row of the tableau. Deal the cards in the pile face-up from left to right as far as they will go, the first card being dealt to the empty space where the pile was picked up. Because there are no more piles to the right of this first pile, the second card dealt at this time goes 'round the corner' to the left pile in the top row. Make all possible moves before picking up the next pile (second from the right on the bottom row). Deal and play as before, again moving to the top row when necessary. Continue with each pile, working along the bottom row first, then the top, so the last pile you pick up and redeal is at the far right of the top row. The game ends once you have dealt the last pile of cards.

Finishing the Game

If you have moved all the cards to the foundations in the correct ascending and descending round-the-corner sequences by suit, you have won.

Tableau for Matrimony

LITTLE SPIDER

Little Spider is a single-pack game of solitaiare in which suit sequences are simultaneously built on the aces and the kings.

Equipment: A pack of playing cards
Rating: Needs concentration
Level of Difficulty: Tough

Setup

Start Little Spider by removing the red aces and black kings from the pack and dealing them face-up to a foundation row. The remaining cards form the stock.

Object of the Game

The object of the game is to build four foundation piles on the aces and kings. The aces are built on in ascending sequence (A, 2, 3 ... J, Q, K) by suit to the kings; the kings are built on in descending sequence (K, Q, J ... 3, 2, A) by suit to the aces.

Playing the Game

Deal eight face-up cards, placing four above and four below the foundations. Cards from the upper row can be placed on any of the foundation as eligible, while cards from the lower row can only be moved to the foundation directly above it. When all possible moves have been made, deal the next set of eight cards from the stock face-up onto the tableau, one on each pile whether it is empty or not. Cards that become exposed when those above them are moved become available for play in their turn. Continue dealing eight cards in this fashion until the stock runs out and all possible moves have been made.

The top cards of all eight upper and lower piles can now be built on any of the foundation cards or placed on any pile in the tableau in ascending or descending sequences, irrespective of suit. (Note that an ace is ranked below a deuce and above a king.) Any space caused by taking away an entire pile is not filled.

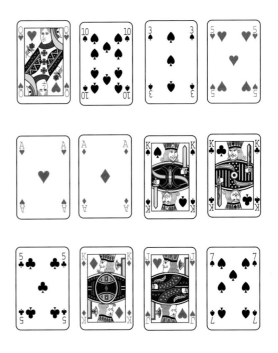

Tableau for Little Spider

Finishing the Game

If you have moved all the cards to the foundation piles in the correct ascending and descending sequences by suit, you have won.

BRITISH SQUARE

In British Square, the plan is to build two types of same-suit sequence. The first ascends from ace to king. Once that is complete, a second set of four kings is placed in a row and, from there, you build the second, descending king-to-ace sequence.

| **Equipment:** Two packs of playing cards
| **Rating:** Needs concentration
| **Level of Difficulty:** Tough

Setup

Start British Square by dealing 16 cards, face-up, in four columns of four overlapping cards each as in the diagram. These cards form the tableau. As the aces appear, place one from each suit above the tableau in a horizontal row, and deal again to the tableau. The aces serve as the foundations for the first, ascending sequence. The remaining cards form the stock.

Object of the Game

The object of the game is to end up with eight foundation piles built in two stages. The first set of foundations is built on the foundation aces of each suit, arranged in ascending sequence (A, 2, 3 … J, Q, K) by suit. When these are complete, the second set of foundations are built, set on four foundation kings of each suit and arranged in descending sequence (K, Q, J … 3, 2, A) by suit.

Playing the Game

The bottom (exposed) card of a column can be played to a foundation where eligible. Or you can place it in an ascending or descending suit sequence on any column of the tableau. Only one card can be moved at a time. The first card placed on a tableau column governs the direction of the sequence and it cannot be reversed. You can, however, change the direction of a sequence, if required, by reversing it onto a suitable card at the bottom of another column. Ascending sequences end with kings, and descending sequences end with aces. The top card of the waste pile or a card from stock can be used to fill the spaces in the tableau.

Deal the stock one at a time, consigning those cards that can't be moved to a foundation or don't fit into a sequence face-up to a waste pile. There is no re-deal allowed.

Tableau for British Square

Finishing the Game

If you have moved all the cards to the foundation piles in the correct ascending and descending sequences by suit, you have won.

Tip

Remember that cards in the tableau that duplicate those in the foundations are needed to build the suit sequence that goes in the opposite direction to the first sequence in the foundation pile. These duplicates will help you to complete the second sequence and win the game.

PENGUIN

The first card dealt in the single-pack game Penguin is called the 'beak'. It has a unique influence on the cards that emerge at the top of the foundation piles that you will form in this rather unusual game.

Equipment: A pack of playing cards
Rating: Needs concentration
Level of Difficulty: Tough

Setup

Start Penguin by dealing the beak first. Continue dealing until you have a tableau of seven columns each containing seven overlapping cards as in the diagram. The beak should be at the top of the first column. Cards of the same rank as the beak are moved to a column of their own to the right of the tableau as they appear to form the foundations (but leave the beak where it is). Replace the foundation card in the tableau by putting the next card to be dealt in its stead.

Object of the Game

The object of the game is to build four foundations, each one by suit and in round-the-corner ascending sequence. The foundations all begin with cards of the same rank as the beak. For example, if the beak is an eight, the sequences will all run 8, 9, 10, J, Q, K, A, 2, 3, 4, 5, 6, 7.

Playing the Game

At any time during the game, you can move a single card face-up from the tableau into the 'cell' above each of the columns. Collectively, these seven cells, which can contain only one card each, are called the 'flipper'. These cards are used as extras to help build the sequences. The advantage of the 'cell' cards is that, being face-up, they make it obvious whether or not you can use them to help complete a sequence. With cards dealt from the pack in the ordinary way, you take a chance on turning up what you need.

In this diagram, the deuce (two) of diamonds is the beak. Accordingly, the foundations are composed of the other three deuces (right).

Exposed cards at the bottom of the columns can be moved to the foundations as eligible. Cards in the tableau can also be built in descending sequences by suit using other exposed cards in the tableau or those from the flipper. Cards can be moved only one at a time, unless they form a sequence, in which case they can be moved as a unit. Only kings or suit sequences starting with a king can fill gaps in the tableau columns.

Finishing the Game

If you have moved all the cards to the foundations in the correct ascending round-the-corner sequence, you have won. The chances of winning are good, despite the challenging nature of the game.

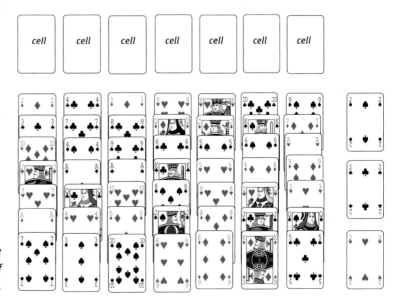

INDEX